LOOKING BACK AT BRITAIN

BREAKING WITH TRADITION

1960s

LOOKING BACK AT BRITAIN

BREAKING WITH TRADITION

1960s

Rose Shepherd

Reader's Digest | gettyimages

CONTENTS

1960s IMAGE GALLERY

FRONT COVER: Police struggle to hold back a crowd of young fans outside Buckingham Palace, London, as the Beatles receive their MBEs on 26 October, 1965.

BACK COVER: A flower-child at the festival held in the grounds of Woburn Abbey in August 1967.

TITLE PAGE: A group of boys having fun in an inner-city adventure playground in May 1968.

OPPOSITE: Shopkeeper Charles Edgar Chorlton smokes over the counter of his pet shop on Derby Street in Bolton, Lancashire, in November 1961.

FOLLOWING PAGES:

Mods ride their scooters along the seafront at Hastings, East Sussex, on 4 August, 1964.

Young fans watching the Rolling Stones in concert at the Wimbledon Palais, London, on 15 August, 1964.

Striking dustmen air their grievances outside Caxton Hall in Westminster in 1969.

Boys of the 3rd Mid-Suffolk Company, Junior Section of the Bury St Edmunds Boys Brigade, tuck into their packed lunches in Kensington Gardens before attending a Brigade rally at the Royal Albert Hall on 22 April, 1967.

IN ALL
PRICES GO UP
WAGES STAY PUT
BARBARA HAS BEEN
INJECTED WITH PRODUCTIVITY
WHAT DOES SHE PRODUCE
THE BIG STICK
DEPOT
WAGE
BASIC
£20 PER
RETURN FOR
FAIR WEEK'S
WORK

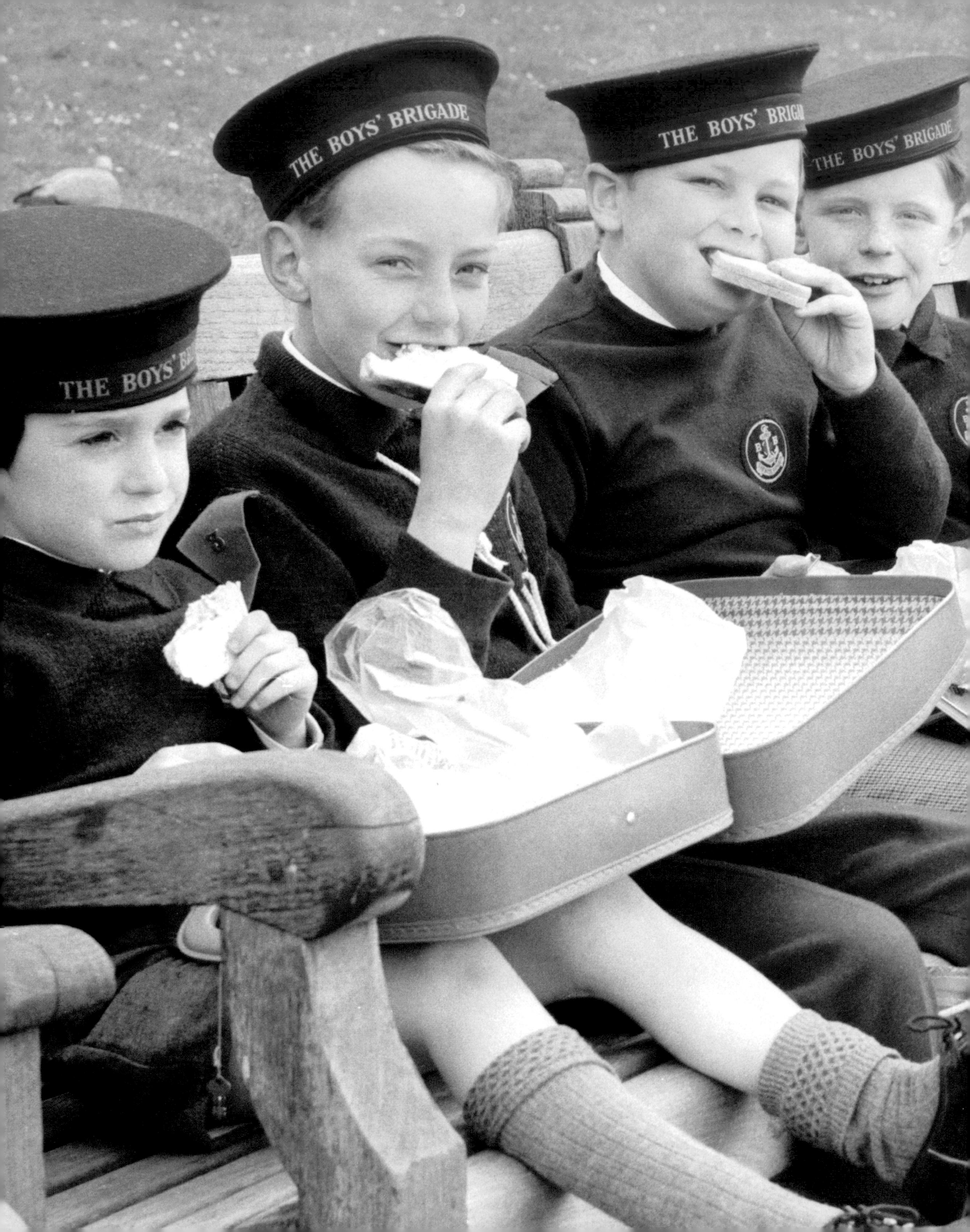

THE FALL
OF MACMILLAN

In 1959 Harold Macmillan led the Conservative Party to electoral victory with the slogan 'Life's Better Under the Conservatives'. Asked by a journalist what might blow his government off course, the urbane Prime Minister responded: 'Events, dear boy, events.' By the autumn of 1963, Macmillan and his administration had been well and truly blown about by events. On 10 October that year, from a bed in the King Edward VII Hospital while the Tory Party Conference was underway in Blackpool, Macmillan announced his decision to stand down. Now in his 70th year, he was a sorry figure, his health and reputation both compromised.

PAY PER VIEW A little boy seems determined to get his money's worth as he watches Andy Pandy on pay television. A sixpenny piece or 'tanner' (2½p) dropped into the slot on the side of this black-and-white set will buy him an hour's viewing.

ON THE VERGE OF CHANGE

Back in 1959, *The Times* had commented: 'People are prosperous, prices are steady, unemployment is low.' But there had ensued years of mixed fortunes. By 1963 the economy was faltering, the Empire was being dismantled and the Conservative government had been tainted by scandal. The 'Bomb' and the 'Soviet Menace' cast shadows over national life. 'Supermac', as Macmillan had been affectionately known, was suffering from prostate trouble, which he mistakenly feared was cancer.

At the time of his resignation, not just a distinguished premiership but an era was drawing to a close. The old, elitist world which Macmillan and his ilk represented was about to give way to a new Britain. The nation was on the cusp of change the like of which it had never seen before. The Sixties were about to swing.

The way we were

The decade did not dawn with a bang. On 1 January, 1960, British citizens had awoken – predictably – to more of the same. As in the 1950s, society was largely settled, class-conscious, family-oriented, neighbourly, conservative, parochial and patriotic, espousing broadly Christian values. Adultery was frowned upon. Divorce carried social stigma, and the process was bitter and adversarial. Abortion and homosexuality were illegal. Justly or unjustly, men would still go to the gallows.

OUT WITH THE OLD
The 1960s would see cityscapes transformed, as older housing was razed in favour of soaring tower blocks to solve burgeoning housing needs. For these Glasgow children (right), their new homes must have seemed something of a 'miracle in the Gorbals': new flats with modern conveniences such as bathrooms replaced some of Britain's most notorious slums. But as time would tell, much that was of architectural, historical and social value was sacrificed in the name of progress. The 'totter' with his horse and his cry of 'rag and bone' was a familiar figure, but would become less so as tower blocks rose in place of demolished streets (below). He was the inspiration for Ray Galton and Alan Simpson's *Steptoe and Son*. Shot through with pathos, the popular sitcom premiered in the BBC Comedy Playhouse slot, starring Wilfred Brambell as Albert and Harry H Corbett as his frustrated son, Harold.

A BOX OF NEW TRICKS
John Selwyn Lloyd, Chancellor of the Exchequer and a personal friend of Harold Macmillan, displays the famous 'dispatch box' before his budget speech on 9 April, 1962. The economy was in trouble. Selwyn Lloyd's 'Little Budget' of July 1961, which had imposed a credit squeeze and pay pause, had been generally regarded as a stinker. He had faithfully carried out Macmillan's policy, and for his efforts would be made a scapegoat. In July 1962, news of his impending sacking was leaked to the press. In all, one-third of cabinet ministers were to fall victim to Macmillan's purge. The Prime Minister took no pleasure in his unprecedented act of carnage, but he was desperate to hold on to power.

The city gent in bowler hat and pinstripe suit, the working man in cloth cap, the bobby on his bicycle, the char lady in overall and headscarf – these were not mere staples of Ealing comedies, they were everyday figures on the street. Girls dressed much like their mothers. Ladies went about in hats and gloves. Fashion trends came down from Paris – material aspirations from American movies. A lot of clothing was still home-made: practically every housewife had a sewing machine and knitting patterns were a staple of women's magazines.

The idealised female form was not stick thin, but shapely, à la Marilyn Monroe. The well-dressed woman routinely pulled on her girdle and braced her bosom with a push-up bra. A product called Wate-On, 'packed with weight-building calories', promised gains of as much as 20 to 30lb (9 to 14kg). 'Skinny women', exhorted the small ads, 'develop a firm, rounded figure. Fill out the curves of bust, arms, hips and legs.' At the start of the decade Weight Watchers, founded by Brooklyn housewife Jean Nidetch, had yet to cross the Atlantic, and slimming was not yet the industry that it would become, but change was on the way: by 1967 an estimated one in ten adults in Britain would be on a diet.

There was crime, of course, there was hardship, there was juvenile delinquency – fuelled, it was suspected, by violence on television. There were racial tensions, there were housing shortages, slums and squalor. But people still answered to the rule of law, to factory hooters and church bells. Sunday was for worship, a quiet day of rest and roast dinners – or of ennui: shops were closed and pub opening hours were short.

In 1960 Cliff Richard was the pop sensation, topping the charts with 'Please Don't Tease'. Children could leave school at 15 and most of them did, but young people had to wait until they were 21 to vote, or to marry without parental consent. National Service would end on 31 December, 1960, but it was not over for some – young men born before 1 September, 1939, could still be called up.

The average house price was £2,530. A sliced loaf cost a shilling (5p). A packet of 20 cigarettes was around five shillings (25p). Increasing earnings fuelled consumerism and a sense of slightly tenuous prosperity. The average income of men over 21 had almost doubled in the decade up to 1961, to a little over £15 a week, and it would continue to rise. By 1962 a third of households had refrigerators; two-thirds had a vacuum-cleaner; such labour-saving appliances as washing-machines and spin-driers were the coming thing. Almost three-quarters of private homes had a television set. Car ownership was also on the rise – from 5,650,000 in 1960 to 9,131,000 five years later. Many of the latest luxuries were bought on the 'never never', as hire purchase put commodities within the reach of more people. While food bills crept up, developing technology brought down the cost of such luxury goods as TVs and radiograms.

Economic angst

Britain was not in recession, but the economy was about to enter a decline. It was not the best of times. It was not the worst of times. It was a period of apparent affluence and underlying malaise. These were years of 'stop-go' economics, as spurts of growth were followed by painful deflationary measures to check price rises. The tax-cutting budget of 1959 had been a vote winner, but by 1960 there were signs that the economy was running into trouble. Consumer demands created an imports vacuum. Britain's economic performance was lacklustre in comparison with its international competitors, not least with that of its former wartime

SPEECH, SPEECH

With his credibility and support waning, Macmillan addresses the public in 1963. He was no tub-thumping orator, nor a naturally gifted speaker, and his upper-class drawl lent itself well to parody by the likes of Peter Cook. But many of his perorations stand as landmarks in history. He was a master of the memorable phrase – what we now call the 'sound bite' – and if his presentation seemed at times bumbling, he was possessed of a keen mind and a dry wit. Neither of these would redeem him in the eyes of the electorate or restore his political fortunes. This was to be his last year as Conservative leader. Ever since contracting pneumonia in his first month at Eton, he had been prone to hypochondria. Now, to add to his difficulties in a climate of scandal and economic woe, he assumed that problems with his prostate were symptomatic of cancer. In October 1963 he announced his decision to stand down.

enemies, Germany and Japan. In July 1961, Chancellor Selwyn Lloyd introduced a 'Little Budget', imposing a credit squeeze, projecting cuts in public spending and announcing a 'pay pause', or wage freeze, for public sector workers that affected millions of state employees.

In March 1962, public dissatisfaction expressed itself in a shock by-election victory for Liberal candidate Eric Lubbock in Orpington, Kent: a Conservative majority of nearly 15,000 was turned into a Liberal majority of 7,800. Four months later, following an unpopular budget, Macmillan sacked Selwyn Lloyd, then within 24 hours he dismissed a third of his Cabinet in what became known as 'the Night of the Long Knives'. The purge sent a message to the public, not of decisive leadership but of desperation. Though it had more than two years of its term yet to serve, the Tory government was clearly on its way out.

'Greater love hath no man than this, than to lay down his friends for his life.'

Liberal MP Jeremy Thorpe speaking in the House of Commons on Macmillan's 'Night of the Long Knives'

THE WIND OF CHANGE BLOWS

Britain had been head of the largest formal Empire in all of history, the 'Mother Country' holding sway over a system of varied dependencies, colonies and dominions, influencing the destiny of the world. But the whole edifice had become insupportable. Macmillan and his Colonial Secretary, Iain Macleod, were anxious to push ahead with decolonisation, to set down what Rudyard Kipling had once termed 'the white man's burden'.

In February 1960, Macmillan addressed a stony-faced South African parliament in Cape Town, speaking of the 'wind of change' blowing through the

STRANGERS ON THE SHORE
Immigrants from the sunny Caribbean arrive at Southampton in 1962 (above left) to what proved to be a chilly reception in a country steeped in colour prejudice. The new arrivals found themselves subject to exploitation, extortionate rents, verbal abuse and even violence, and tended to gravitate towards neighbourhoods where other immigrants had already settled. One such area was Notting Hill in west London, where these four men were photographed in 1960. Two years earlier the area had been the scene of six days of rioting, as white youths armed with iron bars, sticks and bricks went on the rampage. In 1964, the first Notting Hill Carnival was staged as a celebration of black culture. It was to become a great annual tradition, an essential part of London life in an increasingly integrated, multiracial city.

continent of Africa, as more majority black populations claimed the right to self-government. 'Whether we like it or not,' he cautioned, 'this growth of national consciousness is a political fact.' The British government's aim, he told the architects of apartheid, was 'to create a society which respects the rights of individuals – a society in which individual merit, and individual merit alone, is the criterion for a man's advancement, whether political or economic.' This might seem rich, coming from a member of the featherbedded ruling class, a product of Eton and Balliol, but it was also realistic.

In May 1961 South Africa left the Commonwealth, and in June oil-rich Kuwait became the first Persian Gulf Arab state to claim independence from Britain. Iraq challenged the move, claiming Kuwait as part of its territory. When it threatened invasion, British troops were flown out as a deterrent.

The fall-out from independence

The rush to independence, urged on by London, was beginning to resemble a great closing-down sale: 'Everything Must Go!' – Somaliland, Nigeria, Sierra Leone, Tanganyika, the British Cameroons, Jamaica, Trinidad and Tobago, Uganda, Western Samoa, Kenya, Zanzibar …

The impact on white Britons was felt most immediately and acutely by settlers in Africa who faced a stark choice – to return 'home' or to adapt to a new regime. Back in Britain, there were some who found it hard to accept that Britain no longer bestrode the world stage, but to the average man and woman the loss of Empire meant very little.

Immigration was another matter. In 1962, under the pressure of public hostility to an open-door policy, the government introduced the Commonwealth Immigration Act, which restricted the rights of people to migrate to the UK from former colonies. Since most of these colonies were in Africa, Asia and the Caribbean, and since an open border remained with the Republic of Ireland, the legislation had the distinct look of a colour bar. A quota system would favour skilled workers, those assured of employment and the dependants of immigrants already settled in the UK. The months before the Act became law saw an influx of migrants, mostly from the Caribbean, with 50,000 arriving from India and Pakistan and 20,000 from Hong Kong.

Ban the Bomb

Monday, 18 April, 1960, saw a rally of some 100,000 peaceful protesters in Trafalgar Square. For the third successive Easter weekend thousands had made the 52 mile pilgrimage, under the banner of the Campaign for Nuclear Disarmament (CND), from the Atomic Weapons Establishment in Aldermaston, Berkshire, where nuclear physicists were finessing the hydrogen bomb. It was just 15 years since 'Little Boy' and 'Fat Man' had laid waste Hiroshima and Nagasaki. The world had seen what destruction the atomic bomb had wrought. The H-bomb was said to be hundreds of times more powerful.

Speaking at the rally was the Bishop of Southwark, Dr Mervyn Stockwood, and Labour MP Michael Foot, who told the crowd that nuclear weapons threatened the very existence of democracies around the globe, as decisions were being removed from elected bodies to military advisers. The Aldermaston marches were a protest against 'military dictatorship'. Most participants truly believed that they could make a difference. They were wrong.

ON THE MARCH
Protesters from the Campaign for Nuclear Disarmament taking part in the march from the Atomic Weapons Research Establishment at Aldermaston to London in March 1963. This was the fifth year that CND had organised their peaceful protest over the 52 mile route, ending with a rally in Trafalgar Square. The annual demonstrations in the years from 1958 to 1963 were upbeat, diverse gatherings, with marchers spurred on by cheering supporters, songs, jazz and brass bands. They came from all over the country – the banner held aloft by this group pronounces them from Blackburn.

'I hope that, just as he [Macmillan] has spoken for all that is best in Britain by condemning apartheid in South Africa, so he will set an example to the world by renouncing the hydrogen bomb.'

Dr Mervyn Stockwood, Bishop of Southwark, speaking at the CND rally in Trafalgar Square, April 1960

CND PEOPLE

CND protesters came from all walks of life, from priests and politicians to scientists and students. The threat of nuclear annihilation was taken very seriously indeed, and many people were prepared to risk injury and arrest to put across their sincere, principled opposition to nuclear arms. The Labour MP Michael Foot (below left) became a lifelong CND stalwart, along with the philosopher and CND founder Bertrand Russell (below right). The 89-year-old Russell was charged in September 1961 with inciting the public to protest against nuclear weapons. He is seen here, with Lady Russell at his side, talking with CND committee member George Clark during a break in the hearings at Bow Street court. In his autobiography Russell wrote of three passions – 'simple but overwhelmingly strong' – that had governed his life: 'the longing for love, the search for knowledge, and unbearable pity for the suffering of mankind'. His own suffering had included a six-month spell in prison in 1918 for anti-war activities during the First World War. This time, the law treated him with more compassion: a two-month custodial sentence was reduced on appeal to one week, which he spent in the prison hospital. A young supporter in 1966 (right) wears CND sunglasses and assorted badges. A young woman (far right) offers no resistance as police carry her away from a sit-down protest in Parliament Square in 1962.

ROYAL ROMANCE
The engagement of Princess Margaret, the Queen's sister, to the fashionable young photographer Antony Armstrong-Jones – the couple are seen here (right) at the Badminton Horse Trials in April 1960 – was controversial in a society still in thrall to class. The announcement of the betrothal took even the press by surprise. But the wedding day, on 6 May, 1960, was one of great spectacle and national rejoicing, and a degree of informality not often associated with the royal family (left). On the night before the ceremony, crowds slept out to claim their place on the route that the bride would take to Westminster Abbey, and hundreds of thousands more turned out on the day. Princess Anne was one of the bridesmaids, seen here (left) with a posy in one hand and a basket of confetti in the other; the Queen Mother is behind her, alongside the Duchess of Gloucester. Prince Charles, dressed in a kilt, is in the foreground on the far left.

Fairytale wedding

The royal family remained a cherished British institution. Its image had been tarnished by the abdication, in December 1936, of Edward VIII and his subsequent marriage to divorcée Wallis Simpson, but the new royal family, with George VI at its head, had come through the war with flying colours. The image of reliable respectability had been reinforced by Elizabeth, who came to the throne on her father's death in 1952. But her sister, Margaret, had raised further moral and constitutional questions through her engagement to a divorced man and a 'commoner', her father's former equerry, Group Captain Peter Townsend. Under intense pressure, Margaret had broken off the liaison, then in February 1960 she again polarised opinion by her engagement to Antony Armstrong-Jones, a magazine photographer and 'half-commoner', whose barrister father and titled mother had divorced when he was four.

Still, people could not resist a royal wedding. Cheering crowds lined the streets to see Princess Margaret make the journey from Clarence House to Westminster Abbey in a glass coach, accompanied by her brother-in-law, the Duke of Edinburgh. It was the first royal wedding to be televised live in Britain, and more than 20 million people gathered around the nation's 10 million TV sets, owned and rented, in thrall to the fairytale event.

As the Sixties progressed, the couple and their doomed marriage proved to be very much a reflection of changing British society. Both had alcohol-fuelled affairs, and together they courted a set of glamorous, raffish, sometimes downright rascally characters, including ballet dancer Rudolf Nureyev, the actor Peter Sellers, hairdresser Vidal Sassoon and the East End gangsters Reggie and Ronnie Kray.

Regina versus Penguin

'Ask yourself this question ...' Prosecution counsel Mervyn Griffith-Jones was on his feet before an Old Bailey jury, making an appeal to decency and reason. 'Would you approve of your young sons, young daughters – because girls can read as well as boys – reading this book? Is it a book that you would have lying around the house? Is it a book you would wish your wife or servants to read?' The answer, apparently, was yes. On 2 November, 1960, after a five-day hearing, the nine male and three female jurors took just three hours to find Penguin Books not guilty of the charge of obscenity following the publication of the unexpurgated text *Lady Chatterley's Lover* by D H Lawrence.

The ban on Lady Chatterley, enforced in Britain since 1928, was no trivial matter. People had gone to prison for importing the book. A Soho bookseller had been jailed for two months for selling it. Allen Lane, Penguin's founder and chairman, personally risked imprisonment, but he was emboldened by the Obscene Publications Act of 1959, which stated that a book considered obscene by some could still be published, provided it had 'redeeming social merit'. Penguin printed 200,000 copies and sent 12 of them to the Director of Public Prosecutions.

Griffith-Jones's blithe and outdated condescension cannot have helped his case, but a more profound difficulty for the prosecution was a dearth of expert witnesses. Thirty-five erudite speakers were lined up to testify for the defence, including such leading literary figures as E M Forster, Dame Rebecca West, Richard Hoggart and Cecil Day Lewis, poets, critics, editors, academics, a psychiatrist and the Bishop of Woolwich. For the prosecution, Detective Inspector Charles Monahan

NOT IN FRONT OF THE SERVANTS
For many who attended the proceedings, the Lady Chatterley trial was a source of huge entertainment. It was, wrote journalist Bernard Levin, 'a circus so hilarious, fascinating, tense and satisfying that none who sat through all its six days will ever forget them, or begrudge the hardness of the Old Bailey seats'. Particularly rich and memorable were the snobbish and sexist evocations by the judge and prosecuting barrister of factory girls, wives and servants. Presumably it was women like these two (above) – photographed outside a bookshop on Leicester Square on the day of publication, with extra copies in hand to give to friends – whom they wished to protect by a continued ban upon the book. The trial was a classic case of the old-world Establishment clashing with the new sensibilities of modern society – and the new world won hands down.

took the stand. With forensic attention to detail, Gerald Gardiner QC probed the Crown's case. To titters from the public gallery, Mr Griffith-Jones rasped out a litany of what he called 'gratuitous filth'; he picked over and derided Lawrence's prose, which, even at its most lyrical, plainly revolted him. The prosecution was shot through with snobbery. At times, it seemed that the fictional mistress of Wragby Hall herself was on trial for betraying her class through her affair with a lowly gamekeeper. The spectre was raised by Mr Justice Byrne of impressionable factory girls reading this shocking tome in their lunch hour.

> ## 'I feel as if a window has been opened and fresh air has blown right through England.'
> Barbara Barr, stepdaughter of D H Lawrence

Why, thundered *The Times* after the trial, had the prosecution failed to match the defence 'don for don, bishop for bishop'? The truth was that, although the novel – arguably Lawrence's worst – had its detractors, none wanted to join in litigation widely seen as repressive. Assured of the book's literary merit, the public flocked to buy it. On the day that it went on sale, London's largest bookstore, Foyle's, opened its doors to find 400 customers, mostly men, queuing to hand over their three shillings and sixpence (17.5p). Within the first 15 minutes, 300 copies were snapped up. Within a year, 2 million had been sold – more than the Bible.

POPULAR FICTION

Many of the men who flocked to buy *Lady Chatterley's Lover* would have been desperately disappointed by the book. Without the massive publicity created first by its being banned, and second by the court case, Lawrence's novel is unlikely to have been the best-seller it became. Far more to the taste of most male readers were the James Bond novels of Ian Fleming (right), whose seventh Bond book – the short story collection, *For Your Eyes Only* – was published in 1960. The spy genre of fiction became firmly established in this period, playing to the public fascination with Cold War themes. John Le Carré's first novel, *Call for the Dead*, was published in 1960, introducing the character George Smiley. *The Ipcress File*, the first spy novel by Len Deighton, appeared in 1962.

Literature continued to break new ground, and women were well represented among novelists. Edna O'Brien's first novel, *The Country Girls*, appeared in 1960 to great acclaim – it was banned in her native Ireland because of its frank portrayal of sex. Margaret Drabble, an actress with the Royal Shakespeare Company, launched her writing career in 1963 with *A Summer Birdcage*, followed within the decade by *The Millstone* and *Jerusalem the Golden*. Beryl Bainbridge's *A Weekend With Claud* appeared in 1967.

If the Establishment was rocked by the outcome of the Lady Chatterley trial, it had cause to be. Britannia was loosening her stays. A shift was beginning, not just in public mores and morals but in the whole social order. Censorship would relax. There were many who celebrated the liberalisation of British culture. Others could only watch in despair as their country went – in their eyes – to hell in a handcart.

Beyond the Fringe

The early Sixties saw a boom in clever, witty, sometimes savage satire. It was an expression of a new irreverence, which viewed the high and mighty in society, authority figures and traditional values as fair game to be lampooned and, as such, questioned. The trend was driven largely by ex-public schoolboys, products of top

IRREVERENT – AND PROUD OF IT
Richard Ingrams and Christopher Booker, the editors of *Private Eye*, with Willie Rushton who contributed his inimitable wit and clever cartoons, photographed in the magazine's Soho office in March 1963. The three appear relaxed despite facing their first prosecution for libel – for publishing a cartoon by Michael Heath portraying Sir Winston Churchill as 'the greatest dying Englishman'. Sir Winston's son Randolph engaged the services of libel expert Peter Carter-Ruck, who would become a scourge of the satirical publication.

BRIGHT YOUNG THINGS OF SATIRE
The writers and performers of 'Beyond the Fringe' before they became household names (above), from left: Alan Bennett, Peter Cook, Dudley Moore and Jonathan Miller. They were a huge hit at the Edinburgh Festival, marking the start of a new era in satire and comedy. Like the BTF team, the satirical TV show 'That Was The Week That Was' (right), known as TW3 for short, aimed to 'prick the pomposity of public figures'. Regulars on the show included Lance Percival (left), producer Ned Sherrin (third from left), Roy Kinnear (centre), Kenneth Cope (2nd from right), Millicent Martin and David Frost (kneeling). Although it pulled in up to 12 million viewers, TW3 was axed in 1963, after little more than a year on air.

universities. In 1960 Peter Cook and Jonathan Miller, who had shone in Footlights revues at Cambridge University, teamed up with Oxford graduates Dudley Moore and Alan Bennett to present 'Beyond the Fringe' at the Edinburgh Festival. It attracted glowing notices and was brought to London in 1961, where it was a West End hit, drawing audiences from the very bastions that it mocked. The Queen attended one night, as did Macmillan who saw himself impersonated in unflattering fashion by Cook. The Kennedys saw it on Broadway. The point of it was thus somewhat subverted, but nobody seemed to mind.

In October 1961, Cook began a new venture when he opened a nightclub called The Establishment at 18 Greek Street, Soho, with Nicholas Luard, to stage revues in 'Beyond the Fringe' style. At its peak the club attracted more than 11,000

CLEAN UP TV

On 5 May, 1964, Mrs Mary Whitehouse (above) addressed a packed Birmingham Town Hall on the state of modern television. It was, she claimed, undermining family life, promoting violence and attacking Christian values. Having had little effect with personal letters of complaint, the Shropshire teacher had decided to go public and launch a national Clean Up TV Campaign. In 1965, she formed the National Viewers' and Listeners' Association. Her principal target was Hugh Carleton Greene, the modernising director-general of the BBC. Greene consistently refused to speak with her, but she was a thorn in his side: on retirement he hung in his home a nude oil painting of her with five breasts, which he used as a dartboard. Whitehouse might have been more effective had she not seen offence almost everywhere. Many might have agreed with her, for example, over the foul-mouthed Alf Garnett in 'Till Death Us Do Part', but could see little to object to in the children's programme 'Pinky and Perky'. Whitehouse was swimming against a tide of permissiveness, and she swam on until her retirement at the age of 84, saying that God always told her what to do.

members. Among those who paid the two-guinea subscription were novelists Graham Greene and J B Priestley (also a founding member of CND), actor Trevor Howard and virtuoso violinist Yehudi Menuhin.

Eye on the world

Meanwhile, a scurrilous little fortnightly magazine was making waves from grubby offices at another Greek Street address. *Private Eye* was the brainchild of a small group that included editor Richard Ingrams and a fellow Shrewsbury old boy, Willie Rushton, a great wit, cartoonist and raconteur. The first issues were put together in Rushton's bedroom. The magazine was to have been called *Bladder*, in reference to a jester's sheep's bladder, but with uncharacteristic sensitivity the editorial team changed the name when it was learned that someone's granny was suffering from a bladder complaint. It was one of the few punches that the magazine pulled, as its fearless dishing of dirt on politicians, businessmen and traditional organs of the press earned it a scurrilous reputation and a growing number of law suits.

When *Private Eye* came out, Peter Cook expressed himself 'really pissed off' as he had been planning 'a practically identical magazine'. He later bought *Private Eye* for £1,500, then pumped in another £6,000 to keep it alive – and his own. W H Smith would not stock it, but the magazine grew without them, enjoying small-circulation cult status before moving more into the mainstream. It bequeathed to the language such words as 'pseud' and 'poove', and created such characters as archetypal hard-drinking Fleet Street journalist Lunchtime O'Booze and the mythical proprietor Lord Gnome.

In November 1962 the BBC, under new director-general Hugh Carleton Greene, jumped aboard the as-yet small satirical bandwagon when it screened a highly original new series called 'That Was The Week That Was'. The theme song, sung by Millicent Martin, had new words each week to reflect the news. It proceeded with a monologue by host David Frost, then moved on through sketches, songs and studio debate. Journalist Bernard Levin spewed invective. Willie Rushton drew cartoons. Mary Whitehouse deemed the programme 'anti-authority, anti-religious, anti-patriotism, pro-dirt'. Add in the fact that it was funny and this neatly explains its broad appeal.

At the height of its popularity, 'TW3' attracted 12 million viewers, even emptying pubs on a Saturday night as viewers went home to watch it. Nonetheless, at the end of 1963 it was axed by a reluctant Hugh Carleton Greene. He received a knighthood the following year. David Frost closed the final show with the words, 'That was That Was The Week That Was, that was'.

> ## 'It was as a pillar of the Establishment that I yielded to the fascist hyena-like howls to take it off.'

Hugh Carleton Greene, Director-General of the BBC, on the decision to axe 'That Was The Week That Was'

De Gaulle says 'non'

'England is insular and maritime, linked through its trade to very diverse and different countries. In short, the nature and structure of England differs profoundly from those of the continentals … The entry of Britain would completely change the Common Market, which would become a colossal Atlantic grouping under American domination and control.' So spoke French President Charles de Gaulle at a press conference in January 1963, explaining his resistance to Britain joining the six nations of the European Economic Community.

When the EEC was formed in 1957, Britain could have taken a decisive lead. Now Macmillan was reduced to the role of supplicant – and failed supplicant at that. The formal application to join was made in August 1961, and in November de Gaulle came to Britain for talks with Macmillan. Here, de Gaulle expressed his concerns that the EEC would be 'drowned in the Atlantic', and furthermore that Britain would bring in its 'great escort' of Commonwealth countries.

In December 1962, de Gaulle received Macmillan at Rambouillet, a château outside Paris, where he had organised a pheasant shoot. Macmillan bagged 77 birds, but he did not bag EEC membership. De Gaulle's intransigence reduced him, at one point, to tears. 'The poor man to whom I had nothing to give', de Gaulle would later tell his cabinet, 'seemed so sad, so beaten, that I wanted to put my hand on his shoulder and say to him, as in the Edith Piaf song, "Ne pleurez pas, milord".' After the Paris press conference, a humiliated Macmillan wrote in his diary: 'The French always betray you in the end.'

A NATION OF GAMBLERS

The Betting and Gaming Act of 1960 was an entirely well-intentioned piece of legislation, of the sort with which the road to hell is paved. One of the Act's more benign effects, from January 1961, was to allow gambling for small sums in games of skill and chance. Henceforth, sixpences could change hand at whist drives and vicars could hold raffles for the steeple fund without threat of prosecution. As a *Daily Telegraph* editorial put it: 'Weekly bridge clubs, meeting in the local hotel, will no longer have to settle up in the bus shelter.'

The Act also gave the go-ahead for betting shops to open from May 1961. Within six months 10,000 of them had sprung up across the country. It was hoped that, through legalisation of off-course betting for horse-racing and dog-racing, the gambling habits of the country would come under government control, and to that end the Archbishop of Canterbury, Dr Geoffrey Fisher, welcomed the move. There would now be an end to the practice of 'runners' being sent out by bookies to collect stake money from punters.

The Act further authorised the licensing of Bingo clubs across the UK, and with British cinemas in steep decline, many a former picture palace now rang with the calls of 'two fat ladies', 'legs eleven' and 'clickety-click'. There were long waiting-lists for membership, and queues for admission formed round the block. By June 1961, Mecca alone was attracting 150,000 players a day, who soon learned a

HAVING A FLUTTER
A punter studies the odds while waiting to place a bet in a legalised betting shop in June 1961. Some bookies were hesitant at the outset, not sure how the public would react to the innovation. Even when new, the betting shops had a seedy image, with spartan interiors and a mandatory 'dead' (curtained or blacked-out) window, lest the young and impressionable be lured inside. Even so, the new licensed premises promised to be hugely profitable.

GOING TO THE DOGS
On-course bookmakers at West Ham greyhound track in east London. Thanks to the Betting and Gaming Act, steered through Parliament by Home Secretary Rab Butler, off-course bookmakers in betting

shops were legalised in 1961. In a 'mission statement' published by *Sporting Life*, Butler wrote that the Act provided a means for such men to conduct their business without fear of infringing the law. 'If the new laws are to work well, the cooperation of everyone concerned will be required. I am convinced … that the new social experiment will be successful.' The Act was in some ways an enlightened piece of legislation, but a government survey of social change, at the end of 1962, recorded that, partly as a result of the changes, gambling had reached 'stupendous' levels. We had become, said the survey's authors, a nation of debtors, and had entered an era of materialism that expressed itself in 'a grasping after unearned wealth'.

whole new lexicon of Bingo terms. 'Two little ducks', the caller would say, eliciting a response of 'Quack, quack' from the engrossed audience. Callers had to be personable, with the skills to control sometimes rowdy crowds. Many callers developed their own styles, attracting loyal followings, and a night at the Bingo was a night of entertainment, not merely a matter of winning or losing.

This was not how many commentators in the press saw it. According to their lurid accounts, when housewives were not feeding the family's grocery money into the Bingo industry maw, they were dropping it into the slots of fruit machines now legally installed in pubs. In December 1962, a government survey of social change found that the average annual spend on gambling had reached nearly £14 per head of population.

Government predictions

Licking their fingers and holding them to the wind, government forecasters predicted that 'More people will want to move into an outer suburban life, buy cars, educate their children longer, suffer their surgical illnesses in private rooms of hospitals, spend evenings staring at television, spend more, gamble more, buy more washing-machines on hire purchase, take holidays in Italy, lay their own parquet floors, and so on.' They had it right, but they had not foreseen the half.

CRISIS OVER CUBA

The crisis was played out by the USA and USSR, but for a week in 1962 Britain and the rest of the world held its breath as the superpowers came to the brink of nuclear war. For the US government it began on 14 October, when an American reconnaissance plane spotted Soviet missile bases being erected on Fidel Castro's Cuba, capable of targeting the USA. On 22 October, the crisis was made public when President Kennedy ordered a naval blockade of the island and threatened the USSR with attack if any missiles were launched against American soil.

For Britain, the crisis came close to home. In 1961 Macmillan had agreed to a fleet of Polaris submarines being stationed at a US naval base on Scotland's Holy Loch. Overnight they slipped away to prepare for a possible attack on Russia. With these events, it is believed that Macmillan began to lay plans to take his government underground, to hole up in a system of secret bunkers, from there to govern the few survivors who had not been atomised.

FEARS OF NUCLEAR WAR
On 27 October, 1962, members of CND's 'Committee of 100' stage a sit-in in Whitehall, contained by a cordon of police, in protest over the Cuban Missile Crisis. Whether or not the crisis was a great game of bluff between the Kremlin and the White House, for a terrifying week it seemed that the world was on the brink of Armageddon. CND was quick to exploit anti-nuclear sentiments. In a leaflet entitled *Seven Days that Shook the World*, published as the international panic subsided, it argued that 'the British government was not consulted during the world's biggest-ever crisis week ... President Kennedy made his plans first and told Macmillan about them afterward'. Reminding the British public that although the current drama was over, there could be more in the future, it urged: 'Don't just sit back and wait for the next crisis. You have a voice: use it.'

THE SINGLE LIFE – BEDSIT LAND

The journalist Katharine Whitehorn was among the first – and the most witty – to write a newspaper column drawing upon her personal life, distilling broader truths from her own experience. By the 1960s she was married to fellow journalist and aspiring author Gavin Lyall, but she was still able to mine her time as a single girl living in rented lodgings in London – these photos of her were originally taken in the late 1950s for the *Picture Post*. Her 1961 book *Cooking in a Bedsit* reflected the often dispiriting realities of city life for the young, unmarried woman on a low income. The territory was explored by other writers of the era, including Lynn Reid Banks in her 1960 novel *The L-Shaped Room*, which also confronted the taboo of pregnancy outside marriage. Whitehorn's book was full of sound advice for the many single working girls living with a two-ring hob and no fridge, larder or sink for washing-up, who might try a risotto made with packet soup or beat an egg with a knife for want of a whisk. Cooking times, the author warned, did not include 'the time it takes you to find the salt in the suitcase under the bed'. Bedsit houses were still often run by formidable landladies, who did not allow gentlemen callers.

On 28 October, a great, global sigh of relief went up, as Russian leader Nikita Khrushchev agreed to dismantle all the missiles based in Cuba. Praising this 'important contribution to peace', Kennedy promised in return that the US would not invade Cuba, and would lift the blockade on the island.

In the wake of the crisis, the British authorities produced a Civil Defence booklet, designed to help the public to cope with a nuclear strike, 'without scaring them stupid'. Titled 'Advising the Householder on Protection Against Nuclear Attack', it reminded those fleeing their homes to take a travel rug and not to forget their pets. 'If you have to go outside put on gumboots or stout shoes', ran the guidance, 'a hat or headscarf, coat done up to the neck, and gloves.' Confidential government plans envisaged some 5,000 to 6,000 selected staffers leaving their families to their fate. These chosen ones would follow directions to 'headquarters', pausing only to slap some processed cheese between two slices of Wonderloaf, in accordance with the advice to 'take a packed lunch'.

IN THE BLEAK MIDWINTER

Just before Christmas 1962 began what was to be the coldest winter over England and Wales since 1740 – more cruel even than the famously harsh winter of 1947. December was grim enough, with London experiencing two days of the worst fog since the Great Smog of 1952. Then, after three stormy weeks, on 22 December icy easterly winds began to blow, as they would blow for day after day. On Christmas Eve a belt of snow spread south from Scotland. By Boxing Day the whole country was blanketed by snow. There followed, on 29 and 30 December, a blizzard causing snowdrifts 20ft (6m) deep in places not used to such conditions, such as the southwest of England and south Wales. Roads and railways everywhere were impassable. Telephone lines were down. Villages were cut off. Livestock perished when the farmers could not reach their animals.

As always, it was fun at first – at least for children, enjoying snowball fights, toboggans and makeshift sleds. Ponds were transformed into skating rinks. Londoners skied on Hampstead Heath. But the weather was remorseless as the weeks went by. In January, the Thames froze right across in places. Ice formed on the sea, throwing up amazing ice sculptures as ice blocks were dashed against promenades. Birds dropped dead from cold and starvation.

Occasional daytime thaws gave way to frost at night, as temperatures dropped as low as minus 16°F (minus 9°C). Hospitals were kept busy dealing with fractures, as people slipped on treacherous roads and pavements. And the soccer schedule was so hopelessly disrupted by the weather that the football Pools Panel was set up to determine hypothetical results for cancelled games.

At last, on 4 March, a mild south-westerly wind began to blow, bringing rain – and more rain. On 6 March the temperature suddenly shot up to 62°F (17°C). There was flooding to come but the worst of the winter was over, although not soon forgotten by those who had toiled and shivered through it.

FREEZING ON THE BEAT
A policeman wears a mask to protect his throat and lungs against freezing fog in London on New Year's Day, 1963. The unrelenting misery of the 'big freeze' fostered a greater sense of community, as people looked out for their elderly neighbours, clearing paths to their doors and bringing them food and fuel.

THE BIG FREEZE – WINTER 1962–63

FROZEN UP
On 22 January, 1963, boats were locked in their berths by ice at Leigh-on-Sea (left), as men looked out on a scene more reminiscent of the Arctic Circle than the Thames Estuary. In the same month the sea froze for half a mile offshore at Herne Bay, Kent. Birds were dropping from their perches, killed by cold and starvation. Freezing fog posed a frequent hazard.

The bitter winter of 1962-63 was not without its lighter moments. Children enjoyed the novelty of the snow, building snowmen, throwing snowballs and careering down slopes on toboggans. Even some adults made the most of it, like the resourceful skier below hitching a ride through London's Earl's Court on 29 December, 1962. As the pavements were cleared, snow was shovelled into the gutters, where it failed to melt and gradually built into walls, cutting pedestrians off from the roads. Yet even in such appalling winter conditions, buses continued to run. It did not seem to occur to anybody not to make the journey to their place of work or school, if it was at all physically possible.

SNAPSHOTS OF SURVIVAL

In Arctic conditions, Britain struggled to cope. Many rural households were completely snowed in and cut off – for weeks, even months in some of the more remote upland areas. The price of fresh food rocketed as stocks ran low. There were power cuts as electricity lines came down under snow and ice; gas and water pipes burst. Airports were closed, rail travel was disrupted, refuse went uncollected, sporting fixtures were cancelled. The army was brought in to help in places, as on this road in Devon (above), where Royal Marines dig out stranded cars so the snow plough can clear the road. As time went on, in rural areas it was farmers and their livestock who suffered most. Thousands of animals died because farmers were not able to get enough food to them. The RAF did what it could using helicopters to airlift fodder to farmers desperate to keep their animals alive. This Sikorsky S-55 (left) is taking off in January 1963 to deliver bales of hay to sheep on Exmoor; the people on the ground are local villagers who were helping to load the hay into the helicopter. The sheep and cattle at Whipsnade Zoo fared rather better than farm animals stranded out on the moors. Here, keeper Harry Stevens carries a bale of hay for them (bottom right). Meanwhile, a major concern for the public was simply keeping warm in what was said to be the coldest winter for 200 years. With heavily increased demand, fuel for heating was in short supply. These people (top right) are collecting their allocation of 1cwt (50kg) of coke.

THE LIVERPOOL SCENE

There was one place in Britain in the early 1960s where people had no trouble keeping warm: the cellar of number 10 Mathew Street, Liverpool – better known as the Cavern Club.

The Cavern was, in truth, a bit of a dive. It had begun life in 1957 with the aim of becoming Britain's foremost jazz cellar. It hosted skiffle groups throughout the short-lived skiffle craze, but soon began to resonate to a headier beat. By the early sixties it was the hub and spiritual home of the emerging Mersey sound.

CAVERN NIGHTS
Gerry and the Pacemakers performing in Liverpool's Cavern Club, the crucible of 1960s pop (left). The most famous of the Cavern regulars were The Beatles (below), looking young and fresh-faced in February 1961, with Pete Best on drums behind the line-up of George Harrison, Paul McCartney and John Lennon. During 1960 the Silver Beatles, as they then were, played without a regular drummer until that August, when Paul McCartney called Pete Best to sound him out about joining the band. In 1962 Best was dropped, without explanation, in favour of Richard Starkey, aka Ringo Starr, just before the band took off into the stratosphere.

The city boasted more salubrious clubs, but the barrel-vaulted Cavern had an atmosphere of its own. There was a peculiar thrill to walking down the 18 stone steps. Lunch-time sessions were a tremendous draw, and many a Liverpool teenager 'sagged off' school to hear the bands and to dance the 'Cavern Stomp'.

The Beatles played the Cavern almost 300 times. The Swinging Blue Jeans hosted their own guest night. Former choirboy Gerry Marsden and his group the Pacemakers were Cavern regulars. They topped the charts with their first three singles, including their version of an old Rogers and Hammerstein song, 'You'll Never Walk Alone', in the process bequeathing an anthem to the city and one of its famous football clubs. A schoolgirl named Priscilla White, the daughter of a docker and a market stallholder, worked as a lunchtime coat-check attendant. She would grow up to be Cilla Black and, after a brief stint as a Dictaphone typist, storm to the top of the charts in 1964 with 'Anyone Who Had a Heart'.

The Beatles' first recognised chart-toppers were 'From Me to You' and 'She Loves You'. 'Please Please Me' reached the top slot in all but the 'official' Record Retailer chart. Their last performance at the Cavern was in August 1963. They had simply outgrown the venue and were set to take the world by storm.

WILSON WINS THE DAY

THE DEATH OF GAITSKELL
A reader with the broadsheet *Daily Mail* dated 19 January, 1963, the day the death of Labour leader Hugh Gaitskell made banner headlines. John Harris, Labour Party spokesman, reported that doctors had told him Gaitskell had 'put up a tremendous fight for life'. He had become ill with influenza in December, but rallied over Christmas and was declared fit to travel to the USSR on 1 January to meet with Soviet leader Nikita Khrushchev. But he became ill with another virus and was admitted to hospital on 4 January. His kidneys had been affected and attempts to treat him by dialysis were abandoned when it was decided that this was placing too much strain on his heart. It was thanks largely to Gaitskell's efforts to make Labour 'relevant and realistic' that the party stood in good stead for victory in the forthcoming election. Now the way was clear for a new man to take the helm – and whichever of the candidates won, he would be a very different kind of leader.

On 18 January, 1963, Labour Party leader Hugh Gaitskell died aged 56, after a sudden deterioration in a heart condition following bouts of influenza and viral infection. George Brown, the son of a lorry driver, die-hard trade unionist and shadow spokesman on home affairs, plainly saw himself as leader-in-waiting.

Brown was a clever man, by turns personable, pettish and irascible. He was recklessly forthright, frequently drunk – or 'tired and emotional' as *Private Eye* would put it – and did not always behave in a statesmanlike manner. In his later career, while attending a dinner given for the Turkish President in his role as Secretary of State for Foreign and Commonwealth Affairs, Brown lurched to his feet and told the guest of honour, 'You don't want to listen to this bullshit. Let's go and have a drink.' On another occasion, in the middle of the Peruvian national anthem, he asked the robed Cardinal Archbishop of Lima to dance. Brown may have been the most colourful prime minister that Britain never had,

TAKING THE LEAD
Harold Wilson (above left), the new Labour Party leader, with his deputy George Brown (above right) in 1963. Brown was a clever but intemperate man. He had clearly wanted to be head of the party, but his at-times drunken behaviour did not commend him to some of his peers. Gaitskell's death left one of the great 'what ifs' of British political history: what if he had lived to be Prime Minister? He was a very decent man with a passion for social justice, kind by nature, with a sharp intellect. George Brown would recall that Hugh Gaitskell was sensitive, delicate and high-minded: it was Brown's view that Gaitskell wore himself out fighting for what he believed in. By contrast, many would agree with Nye Bevan's assessment of Wilson as dangerously dishonest: 'He isn't a man of principle, but a sheer, absolute careerist, out for himself alone.' In time, this was to become the harsh consensus, but Wilson was above all a pragmatic politician and his achievements were many – not least in keeping Britain out of the Vietnam War. He also carried his party four times to electoral victory.

but the Party needed stability, and his naked desperation for the succession turned even some of his natural allies against him. Not without some misgivings, MPs voted in Harold Wilson instead.

Wilson was from a lower-middle-class background. He was a scholarship student, a product of Wirral Grammar and Jesus College, Oxford. In his Gannex raincoat, with his trademark pipe, his professed love of Huddersfield Town Football Club and of HP Sauce on chips, he stood in refreshing contrast to the effete aristocratic Conservatives with their gentlemen's clubs and grouse shoots. Cometh the hour, cometh the man. And this was Wilson's hour.

THE OPEN ROAD

In the early 1960s, the nation had a complex and comprehensive rail network, largely bequeathed by the Victorians and now under the control of British Rail. There was still great pride among railway workers, who in 1961 numbered 475,000. Many a station platform boasted a garden brimming with flowers, tended by rail staff competing for the prize in annual best-kept station competitions. Then along came Richard Beeching.

Dr Beeching, formerly of ICI, was furnished by Tory Transport Minister Ernest Marples with an office in London's Marylebone Road and a remit to take an axe to the unprofitable railway system. Beeching's plan, called 'The Reshaping of British Railways', was published in March 1963. It proposed the closure of

DR BEECHING TOOK AN AXE ...
... and gave the railways 40 whacks.
Richard Beeching (above) photographed at
East Grinstead Station on 1 October, 1962.
His controversial report on the railways,
published the following spring, advocated
wholesale cuts in the system. Baynards
Station in Surrey (left), which had opened
in 1865, was typical of many of the small
stations scheduled for closure under the
plan. Signalman Geoff Burdfield is pictured
tending the dahlias in one of the station
flowerbeds – railway workers often took
great pride in their stations. Baynards
was on the Horsham-Guildford branch line,
which was for the chop along with other
branch lines up and down the country.

2,361 stations and 5,000 miles of track, without any regard to human or
environmental consequences. Too bad if rural communities were cut off. Too bad
for Wales. Beeching had delivered what the government wanted and his name has
been infamous ever since as the man who slashed the railways.

The road to the future

Yet the rail 'reshaping' was not universally unpopular. The Beeching plan was
judged to be 'brutal, brilliant and right', it was 'lucid and logical'. For the future
now was on the roads.

With car ownership on the rise – from 5,650,000 in 1960 to 11,802,000 in
1970 – there was the promise for motorists of greater mobility as more of the
country went under concrete and tarmac. The first stretch of the M1 had opened
in 1959, with no speed limit, crash barriers or lighting. It had been hailed as a
symbol of progress, and as the diggers carved up the countryside and punched
their way through hillsides, the newspapers and newsreels exulted.

Such was Marples's own enthusiasm for road travel, that he was director of Marples Ridgeway, specialists in road construction, which built, among many things, London's Hammersmith Flyover. When it was suggested that there might be some conflict of interest, he simply passed his shares to his wife.

Along the motorways grew up service stations where travellers could refuel, have a bite and use the toilets. For many these were a great novelty. The architectural historian David Lawrence wrote: 'To take a run up the M1 the first 59 miles for tea and refreshments, tea and a bun, tea and a sandwich, was ... an amazing experience for a lot of people.'

The increase in road travel saw a corresponding increase in road carnage, with accidents reaching their peak in the late 1960s and early 1970s. The breathalyser, introduced by Barbara Castle in 1967, was despised by those who liked to drink and drive, but undoubtedly saved lives.

Ernest Marples introduced yellow lines, parking meters, major roundabouts and seat belts, although it was not yet compulsory to wear these. In 1970 he would become Baron Marples of Wallasey. Then, in 1975, he would leave his Belgravia home and slip surreptitiously out of the country on the night ferry,

MOTORWAYS UNLIMITED
Car ownership was on the increase, and motorways were seen, quite literally, as the way forward. This image from August 1964 (above), of houses in west London cowering under a section of the Chiswick Flyover under construction, shows something of the scale and ambition of the road-building project – and the disregard of people's homes. Conservationists might wring their hands, but roads were being laid over great tracts of countryside, so that vehicles might get at speed from A to B. Such individual mobility was naturally popular with drivers and the appearance of motorway service stations, such as this one on the M6 (right), was welcomed by them. But not everyone was uncritical of the effect that this rapid expansion of road travel was having on the country.

'We are nourishing at immense cost a monster of great potential destructiveness. And yet we love him dearly.'

**Professor Colin Buchanan, in a report of November 1963
on how to mitigate the damage caused by road travel**

having siphoned off most of his millions into Monaco and Lichtenstein. As well as being wanted for tax fraud, he was being sued at the time by the tenants of his slum properties. He never returned to Britain and died in 1978.

The end of steam

With rail travel generally, another Sixties casualty was the steam train, all but phased out by 1968 in favour of electricity and diesel. In London, in 1961, the last trolley-buses gave way to diesel Routemasters. Meanwhile, beneath London's streets, the Victoria Line was being excavated, the first new underground line to be started in the capital for more than 60 years. It opened to passengers in 1968.

THE GREAT TRAIN ROBBERY

On 8 August, 1963, one of the most audacious crimes in Britain's history was committed, when thieves held up the Glasgow to Euston mail train and stole some £2.6 million – worth around £35 million today – in mostly used, untraceable bank notes destined for incineration. At 3am the 'Up Special', on which 75 postal sorters were at work, was halted at a rigged red signal in Buckinghamshire. The 15-strong gang of robbers, in stocking masks and balaclavas, swarmed aboard and offloaded 120 mail and money bags onto a lorry. It was ruthlessly efficient.

Reaction to the robbery showed signs that Britain's moral compass was awry. Sober citizens, who would not have dreamt of applauding a bank hold-up, admired the criminals' daring. They were hailed almost as folk heroes and their story passed into legend. The operation had been brilliantly planned and executed. With no fatalities, there was a sense that the exploit had been victimless. Who cared, after all, about the theft of obsolete folding money?

But the raid had not been victimless. For the family of train driver Jack Mills, who had been coshed over the head with an iron bar, this was bitter. He was permanently disabled by the attack and would never work again. He would die of leukaemia in 1970, before he could find use for a fund belatedly set up for him.

COPS AND ROBBERS

'The Great Train Robbery' – the very epithet conveys admiration and reflects the mixed reaction of the public to the crime. Although people did not exactly approve of the robbery, many did feel a sneaking admiration for the robbers who had pulled it off. The plan was brilliant and almost flawlessly executed – it had the feel of a Hollywood movie plot, and it did later become the subject of books and films. But it was, in truth, a violent crime. Somehow, what had happened to the train driver Jack Mills, left permanently disabled by a blow with an iron bar, did not register on the national consciousness and was overlooked – along with the sympathy he could reasonably have expected from the public. This was not so among the police. Detective Jack Slipper (left), a sergeant in the CID who became popularly known as 'Slipper of the Yard', was one of six men picked by the Flying Squad chief Tommy Butler to track down the robbers. It became Slipper's personal quest to bring the gang to justice, in particular playing a long cat-and-mouse game with jail escapee Ronnie Biggs.

THE GANG APPREHENDED

Just days into the investigation, the police had reports of a suspicious vehicle at Leatherslade Farm, some 30 miles from the scene of the crime. The gang's 'safe house' was not so safe after all, nor had they taken much trouble to cover their tracks. Not just bedding and sleeping bags, but post office sacks and banknote wrappers were found. There were finger-prints on ketchup and beer bottles, and on Monopoly pieces, which incriminated most of the gang. The first arrest was of Roger Cordrey, in Bournemouth; Charlie Wilson, Tommy Wisbey, Jim Hussey, Bob Welch and Ronnie Biggs followed soon after. They were sent to Bedford prison, then to Aylesbury for the trial, which began on 20 January, 1964. By that time, 12 men had been arrested in connection with the crime. Bruce Reynolds, a known armed robber who was the mastermind behind the heist, was not among them – he would be on the run for five years. The photograph below shows three of the suspects being led from court during the trial. Following a guilty verdict, on 16 April Mr Justice Edmund Davies meted out sentences totalling 307 years. Two of the 15 gang members were never caught. The money was never recovered.

SCANDAL UPON SCANDAL

Civil servant William Vassall lived high on the hog, in a flat overlooking the central garden in Dolphin Square, Pimlico. Home touches included expensive antiques, bottles of perfume, women's corsetry catalogues and posters of hirsute rugby players. On his dressing-table sat a toy white poodle, on his bed his 'favourite friend', a cuddly white cheetah. In the closet hung rows of Jaeger suits. In a specially built wooden bookcase dozens of photographs of top-secret documents were concealed, along with a snap of Vassall's boss, Thomas Galbraith.

In 1954 Vassall had been posted to the British Embassy in Moscow, where, according to the ambassador, he had proved 'an obliging little figure who was useful at tea parties'. He was also, as a homosexual, vulnerable to blackmail, and as such was to prove useful and obliging to the KGB.

Back in London, in a new job at the Admiralty, Vassall was able to steal details of the latest developments in defence technology and armaments. When MI5 caught up with him in 1962, the newspapers pandered to public prurience and paranoia. Why, they demanded, had no one noted the security risk that Vassall presented with his sexual proclivities? Did not letters from Galbraith, Civil Lord of the Amiralty, found in the flat, hint at impropriety? Who signed a reference for

TRIAL AND TRIBULATIONS
Stephen Ward (above), a central figure in the Profumo debacle, photographed on 30 July, 1963, while on trial charged with living off the earnings of prostitution. An artist and osteopath, Ward was the son of Arthur Evelyn Ward, Canon of Rochester Cathedral, and counted such famous names as Sir Winston Churchill, Douglas Fairbanks Jnr and Elizabeth Taylor among his clients. He was arrested in Watford on 8 June. His literary agent, Pelham Pound, visited him at Marylebone Lane police station and reported that Ward was 'extremely cheerful' and confident that he would be freed. But his relaxed demeanour in the photograph is deceptive: the following day, as the trial drew to a close, he took an overdose of sleeping pills; he died three days later. Conspiracy theorists have since alleged that he was murdered.

John Profumo, the Secretary of State for War in Macmillan's government, is seen here (left) with his wife, former film star Valerie Hobson, at Sandown Park in March 1963. The photograph was taken before the scandal broke and she looks markedly more relaxed than he does. He would confess his infidelity to her in Venice that Whitsun. The photograph of Christine Keeler (right) was taken in the summer of 1963.

Vassall, enabling him to rent a flat so far beyond his ostensible means?

Vassall was sentenced to 18 years, of which he served ten. A tribunal set up to investigate culpability of officials or ministers cleared Galbraith of complicity. Press reporting of the case relied largely on what Dame Rebecca West called 'misapprehended gossip', but two journalists refused to disclose their 'sources' and were jailed for three and six months. If tabloid editors were disappointed that the hearing threw up nothing salacious, they would soon get their teeth into far juicier fodder.

Of toffs and tarts

In the summer of 1963, a long-brewing scandal broke. The Profumo affair was just that – an affair between a besotted MP and a young woman on the make. Had it not involved so colourful a cast of characters, it might not have seized the public imagination so completely. As it was, the unfolding drama – starring the exotically named Secretary of State for War John Profumo, a Lord, a Soviet spy, a society osteopath (and alleged pimp), two call girls, a gun-toting drug dealer, a vengeful House of Commons rival and a wronged wife – proved irresistible.

Profumo met Christine Keeler in July 1961 at Cliveden, a stately home in Berkshire, where he and his wife, Valerie Hobson, were guests of Lord Astor. Keeler was a guest of osteopath Stephen Ward, who was renting a cottage in the grounds. Profumo and Keeler had a brief and indiscreet liaison, which ended when Profumo was warned that Ward was an associate of Eugene Ivanov, a spy within the Soviet Embassy. Fearing that he had been found out, Profumo wrote to Keeler to break off their relationship, addressing her as 'Darling'.

Profumo's nemesis was Labour MP George Wigg – variously remembered

NOTES ON A SCANDAL
Model and 'showgirl' Mandy Rice-Davies at the centre of a mêlée, with her friend Christine Keeler behind her, in July 1963. Rice-Davies was the former mistress of slum landlord Peter Rackman – he was easy to talk to, she said, and a good listener. She gave evidence at Stephen Ward's trial, and when the prosecuting counsel pointed out that Lord Astor denied having had an affair with her, she famously riposted: 'Well, he would, wouldn't he?'

as 'nasty', 'unpleasant' and 'egregious' – with whom he had fallen out over the equipping of troops sent to Kuwait. With Wigg manoeuvring against him, and with rumours rife, Profumo made a statement to the House of Commons in March 1963 in which he claimed that 'There was no impropriety whatever in my acquaintanceship with Miss Keeler.'

Meanwhile, Christine Keeler – having tried to sell her story to the papers – had skipped to Spain ahead of the trial of a former West Indian boyfriend, who had fired bullets through the window of Ward's flat. Keeler had been in the flat at the time, visiting her friend and fellow good-time girl Mandy Rice-Davies, a former mistress of the notorious slum landlord Peter Rachman. On her return to the UK, Keeler was mobbed by reporters.

Over the Whitsun recess of 1963, Profumo travelled to Venice with his wife, where he confessed to her his infidelity with Keeler. They flew back to London so that he might face the music. On 4 June Profumo submitted his resignation, expressing deep remorse. An anonymous ditty was soon doing the rounds:

'Oh, what have you done?' cried Christine,
You've wrecked the whole party machine!
To lie in the nude may be terribly rude,
But to lie in the House is obscene.'

Four days later, Stephen Ward was charged with living off immoral earnings and conspiring to procure abortions. At his trial, the prosecuting counsel, Mervyn Griffith-Jones – he of the 'wives and servants' gaffe at the Lady Chatterley trial – described Ward as a 'thoroughly filthy fellow'. Ward took an overdose of barbiturates and died on 3 August; he was convicted posthumously.

Political winners and losers

The fall-out from the scandal was quite disproportionate. From a deficit in the polls, Labour soared to a 20 per cent lead. Macmillan's health problems were doubtless exacerbated, as his ailing government was further weakened.

The public appetite for salacious gossip was not yet satisfied. Lurid stories abounded, surrounding the sexual practices of MPs and High Court judges. An official report into the sorry episode – written by Lord Denning, the Master of the Rolls, and published by Her Majesty's Stationery Office – was a sell-out, even though it concluded, disappointingly, that there had been no breach of national security after all. It also failed to identify the 'man in the mask', alleged to be a cabinet minister, said to have served naked at one of Ward's dinner parties.

After quitting politics, John Profumo threw himself into working for an East End charity, helping the underprivileged. He would be awarded the CBE for his charitable works in 1975. In October 1963, Prime Minister Harold Macmillan bowed out. But before then he had one last score to settle, a card up his sleeve that he was determined to play.

THE NATION GOES WITH LABOUR

In October 1963, 'history took a wrong turning and missed a wonderful prime minister'. This, at any rate, was the view of Mollie Butler, staunch wife of Rab (R A) Butler. As Macmillan's deputy, Butler was a logical choice to step into the premier's hand-made John Lobb shoes. But Macmillan, who had narrowly beaten Butler to the top post in 1957, was bent on denying him a second time. Mollie Butler, scenting malice, never spoke to Macmillan again. And as it turned out, Macmillan's scheming did little to help the Conservative Party's fortunes.

MAN OF THE PEOPLE The Labour leader Harold Wilson signs autographs in Wales in 1964. His trademark pipe conveyed the image of a down-to-earth northerner. Behind the scenes, he was said to be partial to Havana cigars.

CLASH OF CULTURES

HEIRS APPARENT

Following Harold Macmillan's resignation the Conservative Party was in turmoil. Who would step into the breach as Prime Minister? Both Lord Home of the Hirsel, seen here (right) relaxing in Scotland in 1963, and Viscount Hailsham (below) quickly threw their hats into the ring. Neither would have been eligible for the post of Prime Minister had not the Peerage Act been passed in the summer of 1963, following a sustained campaign by Anthony Wedgwood Benn to renounce the title of Viscount Stansgate that he had inherited in 1960. It was a provision of the Peerage Act that members of the Upper House had just 12 months from its passage to renounce their peerages, so if Macmillan had delayed his departure Home could have been too late to take his place. Both Home and Hailsham would eventually return to the House of Lords as Life Peers.

The news of Macmillan's resignation caused ferment at the Party Conference in Blackpool. The Leader of the House of Lords, Viscount Hailsham, better known as Quintin Hogg, declared his decision to ditch his peerage in order to stand for office. Hogg was an intellectual lawyer and a pious Anglican, but he was also ebullient and volatile. With an ill-judged speech, he whipped up his supporters into a frenzy that drew comparisons with a Nuremberg rally. The next day he posed for photographers holding a baby. It was a show of vulgarity that cost him the outgoing PM's favour.

Macmillan set his hooded eye upon another peer as his successor – a Scottish earl, Lord Home of the Hirsel. It was decided, by what supporters of Rab Butler called a 'magic circle', that Home should renounce his title and seat in the House of Lords in order to take office. He duly became Sir Alec Douglas Home and on 18 October, 1963, was invited by the Queen, on Macmillan's advice, to form a government. There was still the small matter of him not having a seat in the House of Commons, so on 7 November he stood in a by-election in the safe Tory seat of Kinross and West Perthshire – a seat he would hold until his retirement in 1974.

Iain Macleod, the Leader of the Commons, and Enoch Powell, Minister of Health, were among the ministers who refused to serve under Home, dismissing him as a lightweight. Home himself had confessed that, when reading economic documents, he liked to use matches, moving them about 'to illustrate and simplify the points'. He listed his hobbies as 'shooting, fishing and flower-arranging'. *Private Eye* lampooned him as the kind of half-witted earl who might have stepped out of a P G Wodehouse novel. Although a decent and likeable man, Home was perceived as distant and awkward, one of that clique of Old Etonians who had had their day.

Death of a President

Just a month after Home took over, on 22 November, 1963, US President John F Kennedy was shot dead while travelling in an open car on an official visit to Dallas. The news was greeted in Britain with genuine shock and sadness.

Less than an hour after the assassination, Lee Harvey Oswald was arrested and charged. Oswald in turn was shot, two days later, by nightclub owner Jack Ruby. In the USA, the Warren Commission concluded that Oswald had shot Kennedy, acting alone, but conspiracy theories abounded – the KGB, the Mafia, right-wing fanatics, Fidel Castro and the CIA were variously said to be behind the killing. Even vice-president Lyndon Baines Johnson, who was immediately sworn in as Kennedy's successor, did not escape suspicion. In the UK a committee on 'Who Killed Kennedy?' added its doubt on the official verdict. To ordinary people, the murder was a tragedy – a bright symbol of hope for a better world had been extinguished

'There are two problems in my life. The political ones are insoluble and the economic ones are incomprehensible.'

Sir Alec Douglas-Home, in a speech in January 1964

MAD ABOUT THE BOYS

Who could have foreseen that four fresh-faced working-class lads from Liverpool were about to take Britain and then the world by storm? This photograph of the 'Fab Four' – from right to left, John Lennon, Paul McCartney, George Harrison and Ringo Starr, who took up his place as drummer in August 1962 – was taken in November 1963, just after the start of 'Beatlemania'. The Beatles themselves had little sense that they would be more than just a flash in the pan. Interviewed by the BBC in mid-1963, John Lennon said, 'How long are we going to last? Well, you can't say. You can be big-headed and say, "Yeah, we're going to last 10 years", but as soon as you've said that, you think, "We're lucky if we last three months."' George Harrison expressed the hope that he would have enough money to go into business by the time they flopped. And Ringo confessed that he had always fancied a ladies' hairdressing salon.

A vast market for memorabilia was generated to exploit the Beatles' success. By 1964 a highly successful merchandising campaign was underway, and the bandwagon went on rolling. Much of the stuff – like the towel sported by a Dutch student (below) – was mundane or ephemeral, but some artefacts became valuable collectors' items

Beatlemania

The term 'Beatlemania' was coined in October 1963, after the 'Fab Four' made an appearance on 'Sunday Night at the London Palladium', one of ITV's most popular shows. But the fan phenomenon itself was born earlier in 1963 at the Plaza Ballroom, Wolverhampton, and at the Gaumont. It began in Birmingham and Stoke-on-Trent. At the Astoria, Middlesbrough, and the Globe, Stockton. The Beatles had toured the whole country, playing live in small county towns as well as major cities, and all who saw them can vividly recall being present at the birth of something extraordinary.

On the February night when 'Please Please Me' topped the NME charts, the group had been booked to play the Astoria, Oldham, for the princely fee of £75. In scenes that would be repeated up and down the country, pandemonium broke loose, as shrill, mini-skirted teenage girls thronged the entrance and blocked the road. Inside, when the Beatles took to the stage, the noise was ear-splitting. Weeping and screaming fans surged forwards. Some fainted – or pretended to faint – and were lifted out of the crowd onto the stage. St John's Ambulance volunteers worked to revive those overcome by their emotions.

There were, naturally, those to whom such spectacles were utterly repellent. In an essay entitled 'The Menace of Beatlism', *New Statesman* editor Paul Johnson deplored a 'bottomless pit of vacuity … open, sagging mouths and glazed eyes … hands mindlessly drumming in time to the music … Those who flock around the Beatles … are the least fortunate of their generation, the dull, the idle, the failures – a fearful indictment of our education system. The boys and girls who will be the real leaders and creators of society tomorrow never go to a pop concert. They are, to put it simply, too busy. They are educating themselves.'

What Johnson failed to see – or perhaps feared – was that the Beatles represented a new departure. They were original and exciting, making music that competed with anything from across the Atlantic. It would not be long before the extraordinary talent of the Beatles would be recognised not just by the 'dull', the 'idle' and the 'failures', but also by the political Establishment and the highest in the land. In the Queen's Birthday Honours list of 1965, the Beatles were invited to Buckingham Palace, where they were invested as Members of the British Empire.

Live poets' society

Meanwhile, also around the clubs and coffee bars of Merseyside, three men were plying a different trade. Adrian Henri, Roger McGough and Brian Patten became known as the 'Liverpool poets' and set out to bring poetry to a wider audience, democratising the art form. They were proud to be working class, and took as their subjects ordinary people and everyday life – as well as drawing on popular culture and raising political issues.

The Liverpool poets disdained the literary establishment and were in their element in their home city, far from snooty London. They had a wide variety of influences, including the American Beat poets, particularly Alan Ginsberg to whom Henri dedicated his poem 'Mrs Albion You've Got a Lovely Daughter', and the French symbolists such as Baudelaire, Rimbaud and Mallarmé. Henri

'I have never seen anything like it. Nor heard any noise to approximate the ceaseless, frantic, hysterical scream which met the Beatles when they took to the stage … No one could remain seated. Clutching each other, hurling jelly babies, beating their brows, the youth of Britain surrendered themselves totally.'

From the autobiography of Derek Taylor, the Beatles' press officer

WE LOVE THEM, YEAH, YEAH, YEAH
A fan frenzy in February 1964 outside the ABC TV studios, Teddington, Middlesex (top), where the Beatles were working on a new film. The girls had waited for three hours in the rain, when they were told that the Beatles would not emerge for at least another eight hours. Undeterred, they decided to wait it out at the gate. In March 1965 the Beatles were filming *Help!* in London, where these teenage girls (bottom) were hoping to catch a glimpse of them.

was not just a poet, but also a painter and musician, heading a group called Liverpool Scene. From 1964 Roger McGough was also part of a group – a trio called The Scaffold. The other two members were John Gorman and Mike McGear (real name Peter Michael McCartney, brother of Paul). In 1968 they had a surprise Christmas No.1 with 'Lily the Pink'.

Eating In

In 1960, the British were highly unadventurous eaters. The nation's ideal meal was a starter of tomato soup, a main course of chicken with potatoes, peas and sprouts, followed by trifle. Home cooking and baking were still very much the norm, but from 1961, following the introduction of the Chorleywood process, sliced white bread could be seen in most homes. A fish-and-chip supper, doused in vinegar and salt, was the most popular take-away. Salads were dressed by Heinz.

Five or six times a week the average family sat down to their main meal of the day together. Barely a fifth of groceries expenditure went on convenience foods, but TV advertising was already bent on persuading women that their time was too precious to be spent in the kitchen. Why make rice pudding when you could open

OLD-FASHIONED VALUES
Cheering on your political leaders can be thirsty work. This long line of ladies in hats and pearls are queuing for a cuppa, fresh from the urn, and a slice of cake during a break at the Conservative Party Conference in May 1965. The pop scene is by now in full swing, but the Tory faithful prefer to remain rooted in a more buttoned-up bygone age.

A NEW WAY TO SHOP
Supermarkets were still unfamiliar to most shoppers used to being served over the counter in grocery stores. This gentleman consults a list, probably written by his wife, as he seeks out the items in a supermarket in Northampton in April 1963. After paying at the till he would collect his Green Shield Stamps, which were saved by customers and exchanged for a range of household goods. Engrossed in his list, he appears unaware of another innovation in the brave new world of shopping – a Buyright security camera on top of the shelves. The temptations of self-service, with all the goods laid out to hand, were too great for some light-fingered customers, while others made genuine mistakes. In 1966 the nation watched as Ena Sharples, hatchet-faced pillar of the Coronation Street community, was accused of shoplifting two tins of salmon worth 4s 6d (22.5p) each. She had been seen, in confusion, slipping them into her bag.

a tin of Ambrosia, 'the ten second sweet, delicious to eat'? Why peel, boil then mash potatoes, when you could just add water to a packet of Smash? Why shell peas when Bird's Eye's were 'Sweet as the moment when the pod went pop'? And while some returned from foreign holidays fired with enthusiasm for such exotic dishes as spaghetti bolognese, in Britain spaghetti still came out of a tin and was served up on toast.

Cooking comes to television

The most prominent cook of the day was the extraordinary Fanny Cradock. By the time she hit the nation's TV screens in 1955 she was already three times married – for a while bigamously – although not as yet to her monocled screen 'husband', Johnny, who patiently put up with being bossed and bullied. (The couple eventually married in 1977, after her television career had ended.) She often presented her show in ball gown and tiara, as Johnny hovered at her elbow – and as her idol, Escoffier, was turning in his grave. Her cooking style was baroque and impractical. How many of her viewers were going to attempt 'homard Mélanie', or risk flamed kidneys, or 'green cheese ice cream' involving melted gruyère and a dash of green vegetable colouring? Who would whip up a meringue pagoda?

Earnest and adventurous cooks turned sooner to Robert Carrier in the *Sunday Times* colour section, which was launched by Mark Boxer in 1962. There, they could find recipes for Continental classics, such as boeuf en daube or linguine with clams. The sainted Elizabeth David would be found on a kitchen shelf in the rare household that boasted a pepper mill and a pestle and mortar. But slowly and surely, eating habits were changing. Terence Conran – who launched the home store Habitat in 1964 – predicted that soon every household would own a salad bowl. Even so, the changes were erratic, some for better, some for worse.

Eating Out

In the early 1960s, the restaurant scene was dismal. Readers wrote to *The Good Food Guide* in despair of 'gastronomic deserts'. In gloomy hotel dining-rooms around the country, compliant customers munched their way through fridge-cold, canned pâté with toasted wedges of aerated bread, followed by charred steaks, or trout with almonds, or a stuffed lamb 'guard of honour', rounding off with defrosted lemon and meringue pie or cheese and biscuits.

From May 1966, visitors to London could enjoy a unique new dining experience in the Top of The Tower restaurant on the 36th floor of the new Post Office Tower. As they revolved through 360 degrees every 20 minutes, diners could take in panoramic views of the capital. The menu was rather less impressive than the view. Wildly pretentious, it offered specialities such as 'Les Filets de Sole sur les

COOKING WITH CRADOCK
The inimitable Fanny Cradock posing with one of her preposterous culinary creations at the Ideal Home Exhibition in 1964 (right). Born Phyllis Pechey, she was an ambitious, hard-working self-publicist, who succeeded in becoming one of the first cooks to have a television series. She claimed inspiration from Escoffier and was fond of giving recipes French names. She was an unashamed snob, not afraid to tell the nation in her distinctive gravel voice that she would sooner store a baby than an egg in the 'potty little egg pockets' in her fridge. Yet despite – or because of – her eccentricities, she was eminently watchable, and she did encourage the nation to be more adventurous in the kitchen, inspiring some of today's TV cooks.

In the longer term, the Francophile Terence Conran (left) would have a more profound influence on Britain's cooking habits and home style. He opened the first Habitat in 1964, selling furniture and kitchenware – beanbags, Bauhaus chairs, Sabatier knives, ceramic pasta jars, white china and exotic novelties such as duvets and woks. He then set out in catering with the modest Soup Kitchen and went on to build a restaurant empire and write recipe books. It was Conran's second wife, Shirley, author of *Superwoman*, who famously said that life is too short to stuff a mushroom.

Toits' ('two large Fillets of Sole, one coated with Lobster Sauce and the other with Champagne Sauce, with a Bouchée of Lobster and a Barquette of Caviar'), or 'Entrecôte Double' ('Double Entrecôte garnished with Pommes Anna, Haricots Verts, Céleris braisés and Tomates Clamart, Sauce Chasseur'). The restaurant, managed by Butlins, failed to make it into *The Good Food Guide*.

With their feet more firmly on the ground, long-established chains such as Lyons Corner House and the new Golden Egg catered to all comers at a moderate price. In 1958 the enterprising Sam Alper, a caravan manufacturer, had opened a Little Chef restaurant in Reading, modelled on American roadside diners. From this beginning a new nationwide chain rapidly grew, catering to an increasingly mobile population. Kentucky Fried Chicken arrived in 1963, in Fishergate, Preston, after Mr Ray Allen secured the rights to Colonel Sanders's secret recipe. A taste for Mediterranean 'peasant' food, which had taken root in the 1950s, bore fruit in the opening of some decent brasseries and bistros.

The vegetarian cafeteria Cranks appeared in Soho in 1961, at what would be the epicentre of Swinging London. In 1965 the first Pizza Express opened in Bloomsbury, close to the British Museum, promising authentic, Italian-style pizzas to the accompaniment of jazz. The Mill Inn at Withington, Gloucestershire, started a fad for bar meals served in a basket. Chinese and Indian restaurants and takeaways were an ever more familiar feature of the urban landscape. Between 1960 and 1970, the number of Indian restaurants more than doubled from 500 to 1,200. And if you didn't feel like eating out, there were dried Vesta curries and chow mein, requiring only to be tipped into a pan and boiled up with water.

FUN AND GAMES

Child's play was increasingly adult business. Toy manufacturers were prospering, thanks to new mass production methods, television advertising, and TV and cinema tie-ins. Replica model James Bond Aston Martins, Daleks, Batmobiles and Thunderbirds were all big sellers. Lady Penelope's pink Rolls-Royce, with the number plate 'FAB 1', was available courtesy of Dinky.

QUEUE AT THE PUMPS
A toy filling station in Southall Park, Middlesex, built as part of a 'road-safety training course' for children. A group of boys and girls line up in or on an assortment of toy cars, bicycles and tricycles. In the grown-up world, cars and motorcycles were toys for boys. Although many upper-class women had embraced motoring in its early days – and many women of all classes had learned to drive during the war years – in the mid-1960s only 13 per cent of women held drivers' licences, compared with 56 per cent of men. Reflecting this reality, car advertising portrayed women as passengers, rarely placing them at the wheel.

As children grew more demanding and materialistic, so, too, did their toys. Sindy, 'the doll you love to dress', required ever more outfits to keep up with the latest fashion; and she was not complete without boyfriend Paul and little sister Patch. In 1966 came Action Man, the first doll – or 'action figure' – designed for British boys. He was based on the American doll GI Joe, but was modelled on a Royal marine commando, Roger Johnson. Naturally, he was going to need all the kit of a fighting man in the army, navy or air force: dress uniforms, combat packs, parachute, bivouac, mess tin, first-aid box, weapons, tank … Training, intelligence and equipment manuals were catalogues in all but name. The same year saw the launch of Tiny Tears, a baby doll who cried 'real' tears and wet her nappy.

New fads and crazes

In 1958 an American, Richard Knerr, had reinvented the wheel – or, at any rate, the hoop, turning it out in coloured plastic and branding it the Hula Hoop. Britain in the Sixties saw a real craze for it. Later, another of Knerr's creations would sweep the nation – the Frisbee.

In 1965 engineer Denys Fisher brought out the Spirograph, which enabled the user to create bold and intricate geometric patterns by means of perforated plastic discs and cogs, into which coloured pencils could be inserted. The inspiration for it had come to him while listening to Beethoven's Ninth Symphony. His timing was uncanny, coinciding with the fashion craze for Op Art and geometric prints. The designer John Cavanagh even used Spirograph patterns on black and white crêpe fabric made up into evening dresses.

Some toys directly reflected events in the wider world, such as the Space Race between the USA and USSR. A board game cashed in on Sir Francis Chichester's solo circumnavigation of the world. In 1967 the Triang pedal car was fitted with a seat belt. In 1968 the game Go Car introduced the hazard of a breathalyser test. Happily, there was still plenty of spontaneous play. Boys would throw down coats

OF RAIL AND ROAD
As Dr Beeching worked on his masterplan to 'reshape' the railways, young boys – like these three, pictured in 1962 – still loved electric train sets. But as rail travel increasingly lost out to car and plane, so the train gradually lost its hold on the childish imagination. Meanwhile, the James Bond films, starring Sean Connery in the role of agent 007, were huge hits and it did not take long for toy manufacturers to try to cash in. In 1965 Airfix launched their version of James Bond's Aston Martin DB5, complete with ejector seat and hidden machine guns (below). It was on the Christmas wish list of many boys.

PLAYING MAKE-BELIEVE

Children's play still reinforced gender and racial stereotypes, and nowhere more so than in the games they made up themselves – mothers and fathers, doctors and nurses, cowboys and indians. The little girls above, with their dolls and prams on a street in London's East End, display typical maternal instincts. Children played outside much of the time, climbing trees and grazing hands and knees. These children (left), photographed in 1961, are having fun in a makeshift adventure playground. Typically, the boys show off to the girls, rather than playing with them.

in the park to improvise a goal and kick a football about. Girls group skipped with a length of washing-line, they chalked out grids for hopscotch. The manufacturers and marketers were not quite to have it all their own way.

Piracy on the High Seas

On BBC radio, the Light Programme played a safe mix of new pop and old crooners and balladeers, introduced by respectable presenters such as David Jacobs and Peter Murray. Rock'n'roll was not ignored, but it was limited to around three hours a week. To hear the music that they wanted, young people had to tune to Radio Luxembourg, which broadcast from the Grand Duchy after 7pm.

Then, on 29 March, 1964, a new era began: the first and most popular of the pirate stations, Radio Caroline, started broadcasting from an old passenger ferry off the coast of Harwich, flying a Panamanian flag of convenience. It made stars of

its disc jockeys, including Simon Dee (born Cyril Nicholas Henty-Dodd), Emperor Rosko, Dave Lee Travis and Johnnie Walker.

Caroline was the brainchild of a young Irish entrepreneur, Ronan O'Rahilly, who ran a Soho club called Scene and was agent for pop stars, including the gifted keyboard player and singer Georgie Fame. When the BBC and Radio Luxembourg ignored Fame's music, O'Rahilly decided that if they would not play it, then he would – from an offshore station, with no need for a government licence.

Other pirate ships soon followed. Within 12 months, Radio Caroline was joined by London, Scotland, City, Invicta and others. They pumped out pop music 24 hours a day and attracted audiences in the millions.

In August 1967, despite public protest, the Marine Broadcasting Offences Act closed the legal loophole exploited by the pirates and most of the ship-stations shut down overnight. Radio Caroline continued broadcasting illegally until March 1968, when it was ignominiously hauled into Amsterdam by tugs.

Life aboard the pirate ships on the choppy North Sea was no picnic, but it was an excellent training for pop presenters. Many of the DJs were no sooner thrown out of work than they found themselves more comfortable berths at BBC Radio 1, launched on 30 September, 1967, admittedly in a rather pale imitation of the short-lived, free-spirited buccaneers.

ROCKING THE BOAT
DJ Robbie Dale being filmed aboard the offshore pirate radio ship Caroline for a *World in Action* TV documentary in September 1967. At its most popular, the station attracted a staggering 23 million listeners. Dale was 'Admiral of the Beat Fleet', chief DJ and, with Johnnie Walker, programme controller. Robbie Dale's Diary aired from 6pm till 9pm. Walker, a former car salesman, had the 9pm to midnight spot, in which he introduced 'Johnnie's Jive' and 'Kiss in the Car'. According to a *News of the World* poll, Walker was the most popular of all the pirate DJs.

HOME AND DRY

The BBC radio controller Robin Scott (front centre) pictured with his new line-up of disc-jockeys for Radios 1 and 2. In a major shake-up of BBC radio, the Home Service, Third and Light programmes became Radios 4, 3 and 2, respectively. Radio 1 launched on Saturday, 30 September, 1967, with breakfast-show host Tony Blackburn (front row, right of Scott) playing 'Flowers in the Rain' by The Move (right). Blackburn had been a DJ with pirate radios Caroline and London before joining the BBC. He would host the Radio 1 breakfast show until 1 June, 1973, becoming as famous as many pop stars, known for his corny jokes and boyish grln. In complete contrast was John Peel (back row, far left), who throughout his career gave air time to obscure and groundbreaking bands. Other famous faces in the picture include a youthful Terry Wogan (back row, third from left), pop-picker Alan Freeman (far right) and, in front of Freeman, Ed 'Stewpot' Stewart.

THE NEW LOOK BBC RADIO

GEORGE BEST – A FOOTBALLING LEGEND

The hugely talented and charismatic George Best, winger for Northern Ireland and Manchester United, brought a pop-star glamour to the staid world of soccer. With his long hair and good looks, he was dubbed 'the fifth Beatle'. No player had ever before so captured the public imagination, both on and off the pitch. By the mid-Sixties he was at the height of his powers – fleet and agile, perfectly poised, adept with both feet, with superb dribbling skills and the ability to flash past defenders. He is seen here (bottom) posing with a new Ford Cortina in 1966 and in action against Chelsea (left) in 1968 – the year that he was named European footballer of the year.

The son of a Belfast shipyard worker, George was born on 22 May, 1946, and was discovered at just 15 in his home town by Bob Bishop, a scout for Manchester United. He was signed up in 1961 and turned professional in 1963, aged 17. The 'skinny kid from Belfast' was a slight 5ft 8in tall and 10 stone in weight, but he was a key player in Manchester United's victories in the League Championship in 1965 and 1967, and in the European Cup in 1968. Even today there are those who say that he was the most gifted footballer ever produced in the British Isles – simply the Best. He opened two boutiques in his name and was notorious for his champagne lifestyle, but it was his taste for alcohol that would be his undoing. He was to die before his 60th birthday.

'I spent a lot on booze, birds and fast cars. The rest I squandered.'

George Best, looking back on the high life

RUNAWAY RONNIE
Ronald 'Ronnie' Biggs leaving Aylesbury Police Station under guard. Biggs was a small-time opportunist crook from south London, a bit-part player in the drama of the Great Train Robbery. Had he served his time he would have been a footnote in history, but after escaping over the wall of Wandsworth Prison in July 1965 he became the most famous of them all. He fled first to Paris, where he underwent plastic surgery, then to Australia and finally Brazil. He would be tracked down there in 1974. To the despair of Detective Jack Slipper, Biggs evaded extradition when he made it known that his Brazilian girlfriend, Raimunda de Castro, was pregnant with his child. Biggs traded on his notoriety, peddling souvenir mugs and T-shirts to British tourists, and went on to record with the Sex Pistols in Rio in the punk band's dying throes.

Prison escapes

The trial of the Great Train Robbers in early 1964 played to a packed public gallery. In sentencing them, on 16 April, 1964, Mr Justice Edmund Davies spoke in particular of the train driver Jack Mills, saying: 'Anybody who has seen that nerve-shattered engine driver can have no doubt of the terrifying effect on law-abiding citizens of a concerted assault by armed robbers.' The judge was at pains to send out a message that there was nothing romantic about the crime – these were not Robin Hood and his band of merry men, but a gang of avaricious thugs who were going to jail for a very long time.

The story was reignited when, in August 1964, Charlie Wilson broke out of Birmingham's Winson Green maximum security prison. He was aided by three men who broke into the jail by night and coshed one of the two warders on duty. Another of the train robbers, Ronnie Biggs, escaped from Wandsworth Prison with three other prisoners in July 1965. His escape was more straightfoward – a rope ladder was simply thrown over a wall during an afternoon exercise session. Wilson was on the run for four years before being recaptured in Canada. On his eventual release from prison he moved to the Costa del Sol and allegedly dealt drugs. He was killed by a hitman in 1990. Biggs escaped to Brazil and had 36 years of freedom before returning to Britain and handing himself in, in May 2001.

BRIGHTON ROCKED
In typical spring bank holiday weather, mods gather on the beach at Brighton (above). Over Whitsun weekend, 1964, the town was the scene of skirmishes between rival groups of Mods and Rockers. In the aftermath, two youths were jailed for three months and others were fined. Rockers and Mods kick out at each other on the road (right). Although dangerous, their antics look more playful than vicious. The enmity between the two tribes was played up by the press. This lot are probably more at risk from not wearing helmets than threat of violence. Motorcyclists were not compelled to wear crash helmets until 1973.

We shall fight them on the beaches

On Whit Monday, 1964, there was mayhem on the beach at Brighton, as Mods and Rockers set about each other with belts, chains, stones and burning deckchairs. This was a return match after a pitched battle in Clacton on Easter Monday. Margate, Hastings, Bournemouth, all had hosted such engagements. There were differences between the two tribes – of dress, of music preferences, of mode of transport – which plainly had to be settled.

Rockers were descendants of the 1950s teddy boys. They wore black jeans and leather jackets, and slicked back their hair. They raced their Triumph 500s, Bonnevilles and BSA Gold Stars on Britain's roads trying to hit the magic 100mph

which made them 'ton-up boys'. They hung out in transport cafés, listening to early rock'n'roll on the jukebox. The Mods (Modernists) were part of the burgeoning and narcissistic fashion movement. The 'with-it' male Mod favoured a mohair suit and Ben Sherman button-down shirt, with a US army surplus fishtail parka to keep out the wet British weather. Mods rode Lambretta or Vespa scooters and were immersed in the new music scene. Favourite groups were the Who, the Small Faces, the Yardbirds and the Kinks. The older generation, responding to exaggerated newspaper accounts of the violence, called for the return of National Service – but by 1966 the Mod and Rocker hostilities simply blew over.

WILSON SQUEAKS HOME

At the Labour Party Conference in Scarborough in October 1963, Harold Wilson delivered his most famous oration. Speaking of emerging technology, he warned, 'The Britain that is going to be forged in the white heat of this revolution will be no place for restrictive practices or for outdated methods on either side of industry … Those charged with the control of our affairs must be ready to think and speak in the language of the scientific age.' In contrast to the fusty Conservatives with their Edwardian Establishment mentality, here was a Labour Party squaring up to the challenges of the jet age.

It was a theme to which Wilson would return repeatedly in the run-up to the election of October 1964. The campaign, under the banner 'Let's Go With Labour', lamented '13 wasted years' of Tory rule. Quoting Franklin D Roosevelt, Wilson spoke of 'a government frozen in the ice of its own indifference'. His party, by contrast, would offer 'common sense and common humanity'. The picture that Labour painted was of a country in moral and actual decay, in which national debt was rising by £1m-£2m a day. They pointed to extortionate rents and bullying landlords, high mortgages, homes without baths or even hot water, dingy bedsits, shared lavatories, dilapidated, overcrowded housing, where old-age pensioners and widows were forced to go 'cap in hand' to the National Assistance.

It was a partial rendering of the state of the nation, but it was real enough to be recognised. Even so, the 48-year-old Wilson won by a majority of just four. He

TOWER OF STRENGTH
The Post Office Tower soars over London's Fitzrovia in May 1964 (right). It was the tallest building in Britain at the time. It was officially opened on 8 October, 1965, by Prime Minister Harold Wilson, who made an inaugural telephone call to the Lord Mayor of Birmingham. He unveiled a plaque near the foot of the Tower, then took the lift to the restaurant 540ft above street level. On 19 May, 1966, the Tower was opened to the public by the Postmaster General, Anthony Wedgwood Benn, and Billy Butlin of holiday-camp fame who had the contract to run the Top of the Tower Restaurant. For Tony Benn, the structure symbolised Britain in the 20th century, epitomising the skills of the second Industrial Revolution. The edifice of pre-stressed concrete and glass was a very solid structure. When it survived a bomb blast in 1971, its chief architect, Eric Bedford, commented 'I made it to last, bombers or not.' The restaurant was less robust: it closed in 1980.

and his Chancellor, James Callaghan, inherited an £800 million balance-of-payments deficit.

The death of Churchill

On 24 January, 1965, Sir Winston Churchill died, aged 90. He had suffered a stroke 15 days before. His death was announced at 8am, and almost at once crowds began to gather near his London home. For three days his body lay in state in Westminster Hall; more than 320,000 people filed past to pay their respects.

The funeral was attended by the leaders of 112 nations. As Big Ben struck 9.45 – not to strike again until midnight – the gun carriage bearing the coffin began its slow journey, in bitter cold, through streets lined with silent crowds, to St Paul's Cathedral. After the funeral service, the coffin was taken to Tower Hill and piped aboard the launch *Havengore* for a short voyage up the Thames to Waterloo. From there it was carried by train to Oxfordshire and laid to rest in the parish churchyard at Bladon, close to Churchill's birthplace, Blenheim Palace.

BBC cameras followed the progress of the cortège, and the broadcast, much of it sound only, went around the world. In Britain, 25 million people – over half the population – tuned in. It was reckoned that 350 million around the globe, more than one tenth of the human race, watched the spectacle.

An education revolution

In the run-up to the election, Labour had made much of the poor state of Britain's schools, many of them Victorian, half of them with no inside lavatories, almost half with no playing fields, two-thirds with no adequate science facilities, three-quarters with no library to speak of. The promise was to demolish the old slum schools and to build new ones. And it was not just

TESTING TIMES
The children of Fernbank Primary School in London wait for the order to begin an examination. They seem disciplined and conscientious. Their faces reveal how seriously they take the task in hand. Most crucial to young children's future prospects was the make-or-break 11-plus, which determined whether they would go on to grammar school and from there, perhaps, to university, or be among the majority consigned to an inferior secondary modern school, before starting work at age 15. The burden of parental disappointment and a sense of failure was often acute. Socialists argued for an end to such inequality. Tony Crosland, a former paratrooper appointed Education Secretary by Wilson, presided over a schooling revolution that urged education authorities to move towards the comprehensive system, with schools catering for children of all abilities.

WINSTON CHURCHILL'S FUNERAL

THE LONG GOODBYE

Despite the bitter January cold, people young and old crowd the pavements to watch Sir Winston Churchill's funeral cortège pass by (below). Churchill's widow, Lady Clementine, led the mourners with her children – son Randolph and daughters Mary Soames and Lady Sarah Audley (left). Sir Winston had made it to the age of 90, despite his smoking and drinking habits. He would chew through six to ten Cuban cigars a day, puffing them down to a couple of inches and leaving trails of ash wherever he went. He was an unabashed heavy drinker. On one occasion when a group of Mormons were on a visit to Chartwell, Churchill's home in Kent, one of the visitors said to him: 'The reason I don't drink, Mr Churchill, is because alcohol combines the kick of the antelope with the bite of the viper.' To which Churchill responded: 'All my life I've been searching for a drink like that.' He always asserted that he had taken more out of alcohol than alcohol had taken out of him.

'The Divine Fortune, watching Life's affairs, Justly endowed him with what Fortune may, With sense of Storm and where the centre lay.'

From the tribute of poet-laureate John Masefield to Sir Winston Churchill

WE SHALL NOT SEE HIS LIKE AGAIN
Churchill's coffin is slowly carried on board the train for its journey from Waterloo to Blenheim Palace, pulled by the Battle-of-Britain class locomotive 'Winston Churchill'. The final resting place of the great war-time leader was in Bladon parish churchyard.

At wayside stations along the route thousands of people had gathered to pay their last respects as the train rattled by. The last moments of the BBC's funeral broadcast were given over to Laurence Olivier, who quoted the words of the 17th-century Bishop Joseph Hall upon the Valiant Man: 'He is so balanced with wisdom, that he floats steadily in the midst of all tempests. Deliberate in his purposes; firm in resolution; bold in enterprising; unwearied in achieving; and, howsoever, happy in success: and, if ever he be overcome, his heart yields last.'

bricks and mortar that was to be bulldozed. Labour pledged to 'get rid of the segregation of children into separate schools caused by 11-plus selection', and to reorganise secondary education along comprehensive lines.

Tony Crosland, education secretary from January 1965, was determined to achieve grammar school education for all – by the phasing out of grammar schools. Crosland was passionately opposed to Britain's elitist education system. Of the 95 per cent of children who were not destined for private education, a quarter went to grammar schools with academic teaching, while three-quarters went to secondary modern schools, which they would leave at 15 or 16 equipped for low-paid, low-status work. With the baby-boom generation reaching secondary level, and one child in five still taught in classes of 40 or more, there was a need to recruit 60,000 teachers. The Tories had set in train the move towards comprehensive education, but Crosland now drove the process forward by offering government money to education authorities to go comprehensive. Crosland also despised what he called Britain's 'snobbish, caste-ridden, hierarchical obsession with university status'. He presided over the creation of 30 polytechnics and a rise in student numbers to one in ten young people by 1968.

Wilson Goes to The Country

After Labour's narrow victory in 1964, Wilson discovered the difficulties of governing with a tiny majority. Even so, in the 17 months after the election there was some progress. In 1965 capital punishment was suspended. The Race Relations Act, passed the same year, banned discrimination in public places and in public services, and outlawed incitement to race hatred; on the other hand, the

Commonwealth Immigrants Act tightened the rules on immigration. One of the government's greatest achievements was to lay the foundations of a 'University of the Air' – what would become the Open University. Wilson was popular: his satisfaction rating in some polls topped 60 per cent. He deemed the time ripe for another election in the hope of increasing his majority.

Ted Heath had replaced Sir Alec Douglas Home as Conservative leader. The Tories dubbed themselves the 'party of peacemakers', promising 'Action not Words'. Labour's slogan read 'You know Labour works'. On election night, 31 March, 1966, the government was returned to power with a majority of 96. With this new mandate, Labour ministers prepared to get on with the job of transforming Britain beyond recognition.

JOY AND SORROW
The Conservative leader Edward Heath in larky mode aboard an aircraft during the election campaign in 1966 (right). The sense of celebration is misplaced: Labour were returned to power with a large majority. Wilson's government abolished capital punishment in 1965 for all crimes except treason and piracy, but the change came too late to save James Hanratty, who was hanged in 1962 for the murder on the A6 of Michael John Gregsten. Hanratty's father fought on to clear his son's name, still publicly protesting James's innocence in 1969 (left).

VOCAL POP

VOCAL POPS ★ VOCAL POPS

GIVE IT A SPIN
Record shops such as the HMV store on London's Oxford Street (above, in 1961) were great places to browse and spend time listening to records before buying. As the music industry burgeoned there were ever more groups, records and music styles to choose from. The Animals, from Newcastle, became known for their bluesy sound, in particular Eric Burdon's gritty vocal. They are seen here (right) on the set of 'Ready Steady Go' in 1964 – left to right Chas Chandler, Hilton Valentine, John Steel, Eric Burdon and Alan Price. They struck gold that summer with their cover of the traditional American ballad, 'House of the Rising Sun', which went to No 1 on both sides of the Atlantic.

British artists did not have a monopoly. Bob Dylan was one of the most influential musicians of the decade, initially becoming a star on the vibrant folk scene. This picture (top right) was taken at the BBC TV Centre in June 1965. The next year he went electric – and from saint to sinner for many of his fans, who tried to boo him off stage as he toured Britain with The Band.

MOVING TO A NEW BEAT

Like no decade before, the 1960s created its own soundtrack, defining itself by its music – protest songs, revived rhythm-and-blues, original new pop, songs of peace and love. Much of the creativity of swinging Britain found expression in its music scene. A free-for-all ethos meant that anyone who could sing or play guitar could emerge as a star – and simply to listen was to be a part of it. As the decade matured so did the artists, claiming for themselves more control over their music careers.

MELODY MAKERS
The Rolling Stones (above) having fun on 'Ready Steady Go' in June 1964. At this stage, the band was still mainly covering old blues songs and Brian Jones (left) had not yet been upstaged by the songwriting partnership of Mick Jagger (centre) and Keith Richards (right). Singer Dusty Springfield (top, near right) was born Mary O'Brien and had already had chart success with her brother in The Springfields before launching a solo career in 1963 with 'I Only Want To Be With You'. She was three times voted Top British Female Artist in a *New Musical Express* poll, and was one of very few female British singers to have success in the USA. Lulu (bottom, near right) was a little girl with a big voice. Born Marie McDonald McLaughlin Lawrie, in Glasgow, she had a smash hit with her debut single, 'Shout', at just 15. Singer-songwriter Marianne Faithfull (far right) had her first hit in 1964 with 'As Tears Go By', one of the very first songs penned by Jagger and Richards. Cathy McGowan (on the left, top right) did not sing, but as the cool presenter and face of 'Ready Steady Go' she was as influential as many of the artists of the day. She is pictured with French singer Sylvie Vartan.

HIGHS AND LOWS

Jimi Hendrix (above) was born in America – in Seattle in 1942 – but his career as a musician took off in Britain. In 1966 he was heard by Chas Chandler, bass player with the Animals, playing in a cafe in New York. Chandler – soon to leave the Animals to concentrate on producing – brought him to Britain, just as the psychedelic movement was taking hold. In 1967, the Jimi Hendrix Experience had hits with 'Hey Joe' and 'Purple Haze'. Here, Hendrix is seen playing at the Albert Hall in February 1969. He was a unique guitarist, arguably the greatest ever, drawing an extraordinary range of sound from the electric instrument.

Another great showman, Pete Townshend of the Who, is shown here onstage in October 1966 (right). The Who's single 'My Generation', written by Townshend, became an anthem of the Sixties. It was one of the group's gimmicks to smash their instruments on stage at the end of a show. In similar nihilistic style, Hendrix burned his Fender Stratocaster at the Monterey pop festival in the summer of 1967, later explaining that you sacrifice the things you love. On 18 September, 1970, Hendrix choked to death in his sleep while intoxicated by barbiturates. Eight years later, on 7 September, 1978, the Who's drummer Keith Moon died of an overdose in his sleep.

People try to put us down
Just because we get around
Things they do look awful cold
I hope I die before I get old
This is my generation … my generation, baby

From Pete Townsend's lyrics for 'My Generation'

BUILDING A NEW BRITAIN?

Labour had won the election, but there was no time for basking in victory. The government was beset by problems – the balance of payments looked worse than expected, their prices and incomes policy was unpopular, and a major trade union was threatening to strike. But it was by no means all doom and gloom, for Britain was the trendiest place on Earth to be, wasn't it?

THE SHAPE OF THINGS TO COME Pedestrians in Birmingham's redeveloped city centre in April 1963. The centrepiece of the development was the Bullring Shopping Centre, built at a cost £8 million and officially opened by the Duke of Edinburgh in May 1964.

SOMETHING TO CHEER

When he presented his budget on 1 March, 1966, Chancellor James Callaghan had claimed that the economy was 'reasonably well poised' for expansion, and promised tax rebates for mortgage holders. But following the election at the end of the month, it was clear that the balance of payments was worse than expected. Furthermore, average earnings had risen by almost 10 per cent in the previous year, despite a prices and incomes policy, or 'National Plan', introduced in Labour's first term in office, which aimed for a pay rise 'norm' of 3.5 per cent. That policy was about to be seriously challenged.

On 16 May, 1966, the National Union of Seamen (NUS) went on strike demanding a reduction in their working week from 56 to 40 hours, with overtime pay for weekends. One of the organisers was a Cunard steward and left-wing firebrand named John Prescott – the future Deputy Prime Minister, who came to be known by the nickname 'Two Jags'. A week later, with ports and docks around the country blocked, and with delays to exports worth around £40 million, the government declared a state of emergency. This would enable it to cap food prices, and allow the Royal Navy to take control of and clear the ports. The ship owners would have been ready to settle with the NUS, but the government resisted, since capitulation would have made a nonsense of the pay policy. Eventually a pay deal was reached – in excess of 3.5 per cent – and the strike was called off on 3 July.

The price of the dispute for Wilson was the alienation of some of his left-wing colleagues. He had also raised the spectre of McCarthyism by hinting in the Commons that Communists were at work behind the scenes, then going on to name members of the NUS executive suspected of links with the Communist Party. Nor was it just Cabinet members who were disillusioned. On 'Black Wednesday', 20 July, 1966, Wilson announced a six-month wage and price freeze in an attempt to halt rampant inflation. Was this the same Harold Wilson who, in opposition, had been the champion of the low paid and the trade unions? Fortunately for him, national morale was about to get a massive boost.

World Cup winners

'Oh, we won the cup! We won the cup! Ee-ay-addeo, we won the cup!' On 30 July, 1966, that is precisely what the England football team did and the country came to a halt to watch them do it. Streets and city centres were deserted, as families gathered around their television sets. For the first time since the tournament began in 1930, England had reached the final. Seventy participating countries had been whittled down to England and West Germany.

It was a close run match, with Germany taking an early lead and Geoff Hurst equalising a few minutes later. In the second half, Martin Peters took the lead for England. Then, just 15 seconds from the final whistle, Wolfgang Weber took a free kick, delivering a close-range shot into Gordon Banks's goal. In extra time it was Hurst, again, who scored. The goal was dubious – had the ball crossed the line? – but it was allowed to stand after consultation between the Swiss referee and Soviet linesman. In the closing moments, with some fans believing the game already won, Hurst struck again to make the result decisive. Match commentator Kenneth

ON TOP OF THE WORLD
England soccer captain Bobby Moore is carried shoulder high by his team mates, holding aloft the coveted Jules Rimet Trophy, better known as football's World Cup. In England, if not the entire nation, the win was a cause for great celebration, but it is a sign of a different media age that newpapers of the day did not splash the World Cup victory all over the front page. The achievement was reported on the back page, where sports news traditionally belonged.

THE BEAUTIFUL GAME

On Saturday 30 July, 1966, Bobby Moore leads the England team out onto the pitch at Wembley Stadium to play the game of their lives against West Germany. They were watched by a crowd of 93,000, including the Queen and Prince Philip. Man of the match was England's No.10 Geoff Hurst, scorer of three of England's goals, clashing here (left) with the West German goalkeeper, Hans Tilkowski. It needed 30 minutes of extra time to produce a result, with Hurst's *coup de grâce* coming in the closing moments to give a final score of 4–2. Team manager Alf Ramsey, 'The General', had confidently predicted victory. Before the half-hour of extra time, he was overheard saying to his players, 'Okay, you let it slip. Now start again!' Ramsey remained calm in victory as the rest of the stadium erupted – even the Queen could not conceal her elation. The following year Ramsey received a knighthood in recognition of the achievement. It remains England's only triumph in the tournament.

Wolstenholme caught the goal perfectly in what would become a much-quoted phrase: 'And here comes Hurst … Some people are on the pitch. They think it's all over. It is now!' A few joyful minutes later, Captain Bobby Moore stepped up to the royal box to receive the Jules Rimet Trophy presented by the Queen.

A curious incident with a dog

The presentation was only possible because of a four-year-old mongrel named Pickles. Brazil, the previous holders of the cup, had loaned the famous trophy for public display at an exhibition at Central Hall, Westminster. Three months before the final, on 20 March, it was stolen. Subsequently, the FA chairman, Joe Mears, received demands for money for its safe return, which led to a bungled attempt to retrieve the trophy.

A week after the theft, Thames lighterman David Corbett left his flat to make a call from a pay phone on Beulah Hill in Upper Norwood, southeast London. With him was Pickles, who drew his attention to a newspaper package under a bush. Tearing off the paper, Corbett found 'a woman holding a dish over her head'. Closer inspection revealed inscribed words – 'Germany, Uruguay, Brazil' – and he realised what Pickles had uncovered. 'I've found the World Cup!' shouted Corbett, running indoors to his wife. She was no sports fan, but surely appreciated the £5,000 reward for the trophy's return. When he handed the trophy over to the police, initially Corbett came under suspicion, but fortunately for him he had an alibi. And after England emerged the victors, he received every football fan's dream reward: an invitation to the team's celebratory dinner.

News of the theft had travelled swiftly around the globe attracting much criticism, in particular from Brazil. A spokesman claimed the theft could not have happened there, as even their thieves loved football too much. But in an ironic footnote to the story, it did happen there – in 1983 the original Jules Rimet trophy was stolen from the Brazilian FA headquarters and has not been seen again.

OUT WITH THE OLD

Was there ever a better time than the Sixties to be in the demolition game? 'Watch it come down!' crowed the advertising slogan of contractors Syd Bishop & Sons, as old and 'obsolescent' buildings were levelled to make way for functional new ones. Wilson and his housing minister, Richard Crossman, had promised before the election to build half a million houses a year by 1970. They would fall short of that target, but a programme of slum clearance and rebuilding was accelerated.

In the rush to modernism throughout the decade a significant part of Britain's architectural heritage was obliterated. In 1961, Macmillan had signed the death warrant of Euston Arch, the Doric gateway to Euston railway station, and the splendid Great Hall. There were protests from the recently formed Victorian Society – pleas from the future poet laureate John Betjeman and the architectural historian Niklaus Pevsner – but the monument was razed. Down the road at St Pancras, William Barlow's great train shed and Sir George Gilbert Scott's splendid 19th-century neo-Gothic Midland Grand Hotel might have met the same fate had

VICTORIOUS SOCIETY
The poet John Betjeman was a founder member of the Victorian Society, which campaigned for the preservation and appreciation of Victorian and Edwardian architecture across the country. The Society had formed in 1958 against a background of widespread dislike for all things Victorian. By 1969 it had gained a legal role in the listed building consent system, with the Secretary of State directing that all applications involving demolition should be referred to it for comment. Somewhat to his dismay, Betjeman's name became associated not just with the good but also with the bad and the ugly of Victorian architecture. His friend Sir John Summerson wrote: 'Betjeman has not written even one book about Victorian architecture, nor ever to my knowledge promoted any serious general claims for its qualities. Yet his name has become an illuminant and a sanction; through him, kindliness toward Victorian architecture is permitted to thousands whose habits of mind would drive them in a quite other direction.'

A ROOM WITH A VIEW
A once-handsome London town-house (left) shows obvious signs of decay in the intricate detailing of its doorway. Many fine old buildings were bulldozed in the 1960s to be replaced by tower blocks like Ferrier Point, Canning Town, where Linda Marshall looks out from the balcony of her new 19th-floor flat in July 1969 (above). The cityscape below her is typical not just of London but of cities all over the country, where new tower blocks rose over streets of terraced houses. Whether or not Mrs Marshall was happy with her new home, she was certainly lucky. She had been a resident of Ronan Point, a tower block that collapsed the previous year killing four people.

not a railway employee leaked the plans for its demise. This time conservationists prevailed, but all over the country important landmarks were being flattened, while up rose behemoths such as Centre Point, a 35-storey office block in pre-cast concrete at the end of London's Oxford Street. It would stand empty for 15 years, while developer Harry Hyams sat back and watched its value soar.

Brutal development

The term 'Brutalism' was coined by architectural critic Reyner Banham to describe the style of such concrete structures as the National Theatre and Hayward Gallery on London's South Bank. It was a play on 'beton brut' (raw concrete), a term used by Le Corbusier, pioneer of modern architecture. On the domestic scale, Victorian terraces were rooted out like rotten teeth, to be replaced by tower blocks that were often, indeed, brutish. Vast 'streets in the sky' were built at speed to relieve chronic overcrowding – a growing population was predicted to swell by 18 million by the

FOCAL POINT
Now one of London's most distinctive tower blocks, rising up at the junction of Oxford Street and Charing Cross Road, Centre Point (left) was designed by Richard Robert Siefert and Partners and built between 1962 and 1964. Standing empty for 15 years, it became a symbol of unnecessary and unwanted development.

In most urban neighbourhoods, the local newsagent or street-corner grocer's shop was still an important part of life – it was a social hub, a source of gossip and perhaps of informal credit. But this was changing as terraced houses were demolished and new shopping centres were built. This shop in Leytonstone, East London (right), remains a 'corner shop' only in occupying a corner site. The first-floor hoarding implies it had been a newsagent at some time, but a peek through the window suggests that when this picture was taken, in 1961, it was selling secondhand clothes. Around the corner can be seen other shops in a similar rundown state. Local high streets would come under increasing competition from new shopping centres and supermarkets as the decade progressed.

year 2000. But there was scant regard for architectural or social harmony, or sense of place or history. In what became a national scandal Georgian Bath, a complete period city, suffered wanton destruction when much of its architectural 'undergrowth' was replaced by poor-quality developments. Mediocre modern planning blighted medieval Norwich. In the redevelopment of Gloucester's Westgate area, some of the city's precious half-timbered houses around the cathedral were knocked down to make way for retail chains. And so it went on, north, south, east, west. 'There are people today', complained *The Sunday Times*, 'amassing stupendous fortunes by systematically destroying our historic cities.'

Perhaps the nadir was reached in 1968 when Ronan Point, an East London council block, collapsed with the loss of four lives after being occupied for just two months. Mrs Ivy Hodge had lit the gas under her kettle to make a cup of tea, and literally brought the house down.

'Let no Provincial High Street
Which might be your or my street
Look as it used to do,
But let the chain stores place here
Their miles of black glass facia
And traffic thunder through.'

John Betjeman, from his poem 'Inexpensive Progress'

ALL I WANT IS A HOME SOMEWHERE
Homeless people in November 1962 (left) march on the home of the Tory housing minister, Sir Keith Joseph, calling for empty properties to be requisitioned. Unlived-in houses were an affront to those with no roof over their heads. The decade saw the rise of the Family Squatting Movement, which encouraged the occupation of empty properties and defended the rights of squatters facing eviction or prosecution. In December 1966 a gritty, uncompromising drama-documentary screened in the BBC's 'Wednesday Play' slot brought the plight of the homeless to everyone's attention. *Cathy Come Home* was written by Jeremy Sandford, directed by Ken Loach (below right) and starred Carol White (right) and Ray Brooks. Rarely can a fictional programme have had such a searing effect on the public consciousness. It delivered a scathing indictment of the failure of the welfare system to support families who fell on hard times.

By that time, high rise estates had already become associated with crime and vandalism. Thamesmead, London SE28, one of nine 'new towns' designated in the 1960s, would provide the location for Stanley Kubrick's filming of *A Clockwork Orange*, Anthony Burgess's 1962 tale of social alienation and ultra-violence.

Yet it was by no means all bad. High-rise living was perhaps hardest on the backstreet kids, who could no longer simply step out into their yards or play in their street. But a lot of estates were well run and tower-block flats – which still represented a minority of new housing – were appreciated by many of their tenants, who enjoyed the unprecedented luxury of having a fitted kitchen and modern bathroom, central heating and spectacular views. Furthermore, such high-density vertical development helped to contain urban sprawl, and there is no doubt that the new homes were desperately needed.

'Cathy Come Home'

At the end of 1965 the Child Poverty Action Group, founded six months before by social workers and sociologists, sent a delegation to Downing Street to discuss the plight of 1.25 million children living below the 'poverty line'. While swinging Britain was redefining itself through music, fun and fashion, life remained desperately hard for a minority. 'The existence of poverty in this country today tends to be overlooked', the Group wrote to Harold Wilson. There was evidence that 'at least half a million children … are in homes where there is hardship due to poverty. … Some are the dependent children of women who have lost their husbands through death or desertion. The majority are members of families where the father's earnings are low and there are several children to support.'

A year later, the fictional depiction of the misfortunes of such a family caused public outrage. *Cathy Come Home* followed young couple Cathy and Reg from their early, hopeful days of marriage, through the loss of Reg's work following an accident, and their consequent eviction and separation. It closed with harrowing scenes of the children being taken by Social Services from a hysterical Cathy. The play coincided with the launch of the homeless charity Shelter, founded in the slums of London by radical clergyman Bruce Kenrick, which received an unexpected but welcome boost from the broadcast. The play also established the reputation of Ken Loach as a sensitive and politically committed director,

End of a waking dream

There may at times have been a mean spirit behind the tower blocks of the era, but there was also a genuine enthusiasm and dynamism at work. The new city centre of Birmingham, comprising the Bullring Centre and multi-storey car park, was hailed as real progress when it opened in 1964 and was the envy of other British cities. The Labour boss of Birmingham council, the 'little Caesar' alderman Harry Watton, may have been peremptory when, on a visit to inspect a prototype tower block, he 'ordered' five new tower blocks from Bryant the builders after lingering too long in the hospitality tent, but this was symptomatic of the 'can-do' attitude of the day. And then there was T Dan Smith, aka 'Mr Newcastle'.

A working-class lad from Wallsend, Smith became leader of Newcastle City Council in the mid 1960s. He dreamed of creating a vibrant modern city, 'free and beautiful' – the Milan, the Manhattan, the Brasilia of the North. Smith was a tireless champion of a depressed region, a twinkling, charismatic character with a romantic dream. Much of Newcastle's city centre was redeveloped during his tenure, but on a personal level his dream came to a sad end when, in 1974, he was jailed on charges of corruption, accused of taking bribes from Yorkshire architect John Poulson.

In the longer term, the relative success of Sixties' developments varied hugely. In 1995 Richard Siefert's once-reviled Centre Point was granted Grade Two listing, with the Royal Fine Art Commission praising its 'elegance worthy of a Wren steeple'. In contrast, in 2000 Birmingham's Bullring went the way of Euston Arch.

ABERFAN – A VILLAGE TRAGEDY

It was 9.25am on Friday, 21 October, 1966, when the call came through to the police at Merthyr Tydfil, South Wales. 'I have been asked to inform you that there has been a landslide at Pantglas. The tip has come down on the school.' These terse words signified a tragedy of unimaginable proportions. At 9.15, as the pupils of Pantglas Junior School in Aberfan were sitting down to their lessons on the last day before the half-term holiday, the Merthyr Vale Colliery tip crashed down the mountainside. Waves of coal waste, stones and slurry snapped trees, crashed through roofs, smashed masonry and shattered glass. It demolished 11 cottages, but far worse, it engulfed the school. In the silence that followed, one witness would recall, you could not hear a bird, could not hear a child.

'BURIED ALIVE BY THE NCB'
Villagers and rescue workers do what they can in the desperate rescue operation at Pantglas School in Aberfan, but only 25 of the children came out of the school alive. One pupil would later tell how the fire brigade found him after about 90 minutes. 'I heard cries and screams, but I couldn't move. The desk was jammed into my stomach and my leg was under the radiator. The little girl next to me was dead and her head was on my shoulder.'

Another child remembered: 'I could hear men's voices but I didn't know what they were doing or where they were … then this voice was asking me if I could see daylight … and then I was dug out. I was passed through a chain of men, out through a window and into the yard and handed to the policeman, who carried me to the side of a wall where he placed me on the ground … I looked back at the school and I just couldn't believe what had happened. It was completely flat.'

THE FACE OF GRIEF

'The women were already there, like stone they were, clawing at the filth. It was like a black river – some had no skin left on their hands.' So recalled one of the miners called back up to the surface to join the desperate rescue operation at Pantglas School in Aberfan. 'Miners are a tough breed, we don't show our feelings, but some of the lads broke down.'

Miners just beginning their day's shift were called back up to the surface, where they were confronted by the sight of desperate mothers clawing with black and bleeding fingers at the tons of debris. A rescue operation was swiftly mounted, and as news spread helpers poured in. Teams worked hand to hand with buckets. Mechanical diggers went into operation. Here a broken doll might surface, there a child's book. From time to time there would be calls for hush, then frantic spadework would ensue.

The Red Cross was on the scene, and the Salvation Army, giving out hot drinks and what little comfort they could. By the Saturday morning, the miners had been labouring for 24 hours and some 2,000 volunteers were at the site. By the afternoon, 2,500 helpers were toiling in the rain, with a fearful eye on what was left of the unstable tip.

A mortuary was set up in Bethania Chapel and the grim business of identifying bodies began. Of the 144 who lost their lives, 116 were children. The body of the deputy headmaster was found embracing five of his young charges. Not quite all of the classrooms had been swamped: some casualties were brought out alive and a few walked to safety unscathed. But virtually an entire generation of Aberfan's children had been killed.

The mayor of Merthyr immediately launched a Disaster Fund, and on 26 October a Tribunal was appointed to inquire into the circumstances of the landslide. National Coal Board specialists began to talk of a mountain spring under the tip. In a television interview, the NCB chairman Lord Robens revealed, 'We have discovered water welling up in the virtual centre of the tip – a natural spring, which was completely unknown. This spring has been pouring its water into the centre of the tip, producing what an official has described as a water bomb.' Enraged villagers responded that the NCB must have known about the spring, since 'everyone in the village did'. Besides, one had only to look at the Ordnance Survey map of the area.

The aftermath

At an inquest on 30 of the children, as the Merthyr coroner began to read the roll call of the dead, there were shouts of 'Murderers!' One father, when his child's name was read out and the cause of death stated as 'asphyxia and multiple injuries', called out: 'No, Sir. Buried alive by the National Coal Board.' A woman cried, 'They have killed our children!' The coroner responded, 'I know your grief is such that you may not be realising what you are saying.' The father was implacable: 'I want it recorded, "Buried alive by the National Coal Board."' On 3 August, 1967, the findings of the Tribunal were made public and left no doubt that the National Coal Board was to blame for the disaster.

> '**The Aberfan Disaster is a terrifying tale of bungling ineptitude by many men charged with tasks for which they were totally unfitted, of failure to heed clear warnings, and of total lack of direction from above ... Blame for the disaster rests upon the National Coal Board.**'
>
> **From the report of the Tribunal inquiry into the Aberfan Disaster**

Meanwhile, the Disaster Fund, which had closed in January 1967, had amassed an unprecedented £1,750,000, amid concerns of villagers and donors as to how the money would be used. Some physical and emotional rehabilitation was achieved through local projects and pay-outs, but money was not much of a salve. The writer Laurie Lee, who visited in the autumn of 1967, recalled a community in deep trauma, describing the fund as 'sprawling over the village like some great golden monster, which no one could tame or put to use'. The NCB found a use for it – it dipped in and took £150,000 for the removal of what remained of the coal tip.

From the day of the horrific event, the name Aberfan became synonymous with heartbreak. Laurie Lee reported hearing 'a village chorus rising all day from the streets and pubs, a kind of compulsive recitation of tragedy, perpetual telling and retelling the story ... Most of them are still living in a state of shock, in a village which remains an open wound.'

Despite the damning judgment of the Tribunal, in the wake of the Aberfan disaster no member of the National Coal Board was prosecuted, sacked or even demoted. Lord Robens's offer of resignation was rejected. In 1969 his Lordship would be invited by Labour Minister Barbara Castle to chair a committee on health and safety at work.

STRICKEN TANKER

Thick black smoke billows from the *Torrey Canyon* on 29 March, 1967 (above), after RAF Buccaneers and Hunters bombarded it with explosive. This was the final attempt to deal with the supertanker, which had been leaking crude oil into the sea since it ran aground 11 days earlier on Pollard Rock in the Seven Stones Reef off Land's End, Cornwall. An attempt was made to float the stranded tanker off the rocks, but this left it broken in two and defenceless against the pounding of the waves, as its deadly cargo continued to spill into the sea. The oil washed ashore onto the Cornish coastline and also polluted the beaches of Normandy and Brittany. In all, some 120 miles of coast in Cornwall and 50 miles in France were contaminated. Marine life, birds, fishing and the holiday industry were all under threat. An estimated 15,000 sea birds were killed. In the event, it was not just the vast oil slick that caused major environmental damage, but also the way the disaster was handled. In fact, British experts have calculated that the chemical detergents that were used to 'cleanse' the sea were responsible for as much as 90 per cent of the damage to plant and animal life. Left to herself, it has been argued, Nature would have done a far better job of cleaning up the mess.

TRIALS AT SEA

At the end of May 1967, Francis Chichester made history when he became the first person to sail solo around the globe. History of a very different kind had been made two months earlier. On 18 March, an environmental catastrophe began to unfold when the *Torrey Canyon*, one of the first oil supertankers, struck the Seven Stones Reef between the Scilly Isles and Land's End. As its cargo of 120,000 tons of crude oil leaked into the sea, witnesses reported an overpowering stench as brown, churning waters coated the beaches with sludge. Oil oozed up estuaries and into harbours. With no effective plan to deal with such an event, a committee was set up under the chairmanship of the government's scientific advisor, Sir Solly Zuckerman. He had advised on bombing strategy in the war and was therefore an expert in 'the macabre and fascinating science of destruction'.

The first 'remedy' was to spray the shoreline with thousands of gallons of industrial detergent in the hope that it would disperse the oil, but the toxic chemicals only destroyed still more marine life. Next, attempts were made to float the vessel off the reef. This ended with the loss of one life, and the ship began to break up. Finally, at first light on 29 March, RAF bombers pounded the stricken ship with explosives in an effort to burn off the last of the oil and sink it. Sightseers gathered on the cliffs to watch the spectacle. It later emerged that a number of the bombs dropped contained napalm – a mixture of petrol and chemical thickener – then in use by the Americans in Vietnam. Napalm could cause terrible injuries because it adhered to skin as it was burning. There were those who wondered for what contingency Britain had stockpiled such weapons.

SINGLE-HANDED SAILOR
Just before 10.00pm, on 28 May, 1967, Francis Chichester sailed into the port of Plymouth on his yacht *Gypsy Moth IV*, at the end of an epic solo navigation of the globe. He had spent nine months and a day between the lonely sea and the sky, and was now the first and so far only man to sail single-handed round the world. He had made only one stop, in Sydney, Australia. His tenacity impressed the nation – the smiling crowds below are typical of the 250,000 people who turned out to welcome the 65-year-old adventurer home. In July, Chichester was dubbed Sir Francis by the Queen at Greenwich, using Sir Francis Drake's sword.

THE SUMMER OF LOVE

In the balmy days of summer 1967, the air was thick with talk of peace and love, with a heady mix of idealism, mystification, high-minded cant and cannabis. While the men in grey suits were steering the ship of state on to the rocks as surely as Captain Pastrengo Rugiati had steered the *Torrey Canyon*, the Beautiful People, the Flower Children, were going to change the world by magical means.

Old taboos were lifting against a background of liberal reform. The contraceptive pill, first made available in Family Planning clinics early in the decade, encouraged more sexual freedom. In July 1967, following the passing of the Sexual Offences Act, homosexuality between consenting adults in private ceased to be a crime, although the age of consent was set at 21, five years above that for heterosexual sex. Liberal backbencher David Steel pushed through his bitterly contested private member's bill on abortion. The Abortion Act legalised termination within the first 28 weeks of pregnancy, on the condition that two doctors confirm its medical or psychological necessity. It would come into effect in April 1968, and put an end to the horrors of 'backstreet' abortions. A bill to relax divorce laws failed for lack of time in the same parliamentary session.

SUMMER HAZE
'How does it feel to be one of the beautiful people?' sang the Beatles in 'Baby You're a Rich Man'. Pretty laid back, to judge by these young hippies at the Festival of the Flower Children (left), held at Woburn Abbey in August 1967, the height of the Summer of Love. An air of ennui seems to hang over all, but there were some fireworks when the band Marmalade threw lighted sparklers into the crowd and they were showered with flowers from a hot-air balloon. Eric Burdon sang 'San Francisco Nights'. Other bands included the Bee Gees, Small Faces and Zoot Money. A striking aspect of the scene from today's viewpoint is the almost complete lack of alcohol and snack foods. The hippies below are taking part in a rally in Hyde Park for the legalisation of pot.

In music, literature and art, a surge of creativity was fuelled by drugs and the drugs culture. In June, the Beatles released what would four decades later be voted the best album of all time. *Sgt Pepper's Lonely Hearts Club Band* was a highly original mix of psychedelia and vaudeville, with a cover by Pop Art star Peter Blake, featuring a collage of cut-outs of famous people, including Marlon Brando and Karl Marx (the original design included Jesus and Hitler, too). It was widely believed that the song 'Lucy in the Sky with Diamonds' was about LSD – the hallucinogenic lysergic acid diethylamide, or simply 'acid' – although John Lennon insisted that it was inspired by a painting by his son, Julian. Certainly, other albums of the day – such as the Rolling Stones's *Their Satanic Majesties* and Pink Floyd's *Piper at the Gates of Dawn* – seemed infused by the atmosphere of drugs.

Setting an example

In June, their satanic majesties Mick Jagger and Keith Richards appeared in court on charges of drug possession, after police raided Richards's Sussex home on a tip-off from the *News of the World*. Reports of the raid claimed that Jagger's then girlfriend, Marianne Faithfull, was found naked, swathed in a fur rug. In Jagger's

ON THE ENLIGHTENMENT TRAIL
The Beatles and their partners in March 1968, photographed at an ashram in Rishikesh, India, with Maharishi Mahesh Yogi and other seekers for enlightenment through transcendental meditation. Starting third from left in the front row are: Ringo Starr, his wife Maureen, Jane Asher, Paul McCartney, George Harrison and his wife, the model Pattie Boyd, Cynthia and John Lennon. McCartney was briefly engaged to the red-headed actress Asher, before meeting his future wife Linda Eastman. The group's association with the great guru lasted only from August 1967 until the following April, when the visit to India ended with some kind of disagreement. Back in Britain they declared themselves no longer his spiritual followers, and John Lennon penned a song – which he was persuaded to change by the others – with the lines: 'Maharishi – what have you done? You made a fool of everyone.'

coat pocket were a few amphetamines, which he claimed to have bought legally in Italy. An ashtray revealed traces of cannabis. In court, both men were found guilty and it was decided to make an example of them. Richards was sentenced to a year in prison and fined £500. Jagger was sentenced to three months and fined £200.

Support for the 24-year-old musicians came from an unlikely quarter. In an editorial in *The Times* headlined 'Who Breaks a Butterfly on a Wheel?' (from Alexander Pope's 'Epistle to Dr Arbuthnot'), the paper's editor, William Rees-Mogg, commented that this was 'as mild a drug case as can ever have been brought before the courts … There must remain a suspicion … that Mr Jagger received a more severe sentence than would have been thought proper for any purely anonymous young man.' In the event, both men spent just one night at her Majesty's pleasure – Jagger in Brixton Prison and Richards in Wormwood Scrubs.

Festivals and flower power

Meanwhile, in West Coast America, birthplace of the hippy counterculture, the first pop festival – or 'love-in' – was held in Monterey, California. The Animals and the Who played on the same bill as Jefferson Airplane and Grateful Dead. In a dreamy little ditty that became a monster hit, Scott McKenzie advised anyone who might be going to San Francisco to 'be sure to wear some flowers in your hair'. In the same spirit, Woburn Abbey hosted the Festival of the Flower Children,

attracting 25,000 young hippies from all over Europe. The grounds of the stately home were clothed in a sea of cheesecloth, diaphanous blouses and loon trousers, kaftans, headbands and beads. As John Lennon would say looking back: 'What did we do in the Sixties? We dressed up.' Some might have added dropped acid and, in some instances, dropped out. But most of those long-haired festival-goers were recreational weekend hippies with regular jobs.

In July, *The Times* courted further controversy when it carried a full-page advertisement declaring that 'The law against marijuana is immoral in principle and unworkable in practice'. Sixty-five signatories put their names to the campaign, including MPs, doctors, Nobel laureate scientists and, more famously, photographer David Bailey, novelist Graham Greene and the Beatles.

Drugs were in the news again in August, when the Beatles travelled to Bangor for a first audience with the Maharishi Mahesh Yogi at the International Meditation Society. While there, they received a call to tell them that their manager, Brian Epstein, was dead from an accidental overdose of sleeping pills.

The return of trouble and strife

As summer gave way to autumn, back in the real world miseries were mounting. In June, Israel had triumphed over Egypt, Syria and Jordan in the Six-Day War and this led to an oil embargo being imposed on Britain by Iraq and Kuwait for suspected complicity with the Israelis. The disruption of oil supplies put added pressure on both the balance of payments and on sterling.

In September, first in Liverpool, then Manchester, Hull and London, the dockers walked out in protest at their casual employment status. As one Merseyside docker explained it: 'We were put in pens on the docks, and you were hired with a tap on the shoulder. If your face didn't fit, there was no work. If you were picked, you worked the morning, then you were back in the pens at lunch.' These men put in long and arduous hours with compulsory overtime in rotten conditions, without even decent toilet facilities. The strike went on for six weeks, goods for export piled up, before the strikers' grievances were addressed.

On 25 October, vets confirmed an outbreak of foot and mouth disease among pigs on a farm in Oswestry, Shropshire. The attempt to halt the epidemic resulted in nine months of carnage with the slaughter of 450,000 animals.

There was more dire news on 5 November when an express train travelling from Hastings to Charing Cross crashed off the rails near Hither Green, south London, killing 49 people and injuring 78. One survivor told how the lights had gone out in the carriage just before it turned over and scraped along on its side. 'Everyone was clutching on to one another. There were some terrible screams.' Among those who escaped unscathed were pop star Robin Gibb of the Bee Gees and his wife, Molly. A fractured rail was found to be the cause of the accident, and new rail specifications were introduced.

The pound in your pocket

Not surprisingly with so much going wrong, Labour's popularity was waning. It lost by-elections in Cambridge and Walthamstow West in late September, and in Hamilton in early November. The party had been afflicted throughout its time in office with what Wilson called an 'aching tooth' – the weak pound.

After the seamen's strike in 1966, pressure to devalue had been resisted, but the dockers' strike tipped the government over the edge. On 18 November, dollar parity of sterling was reduced from $2.80 to $2.40. Harold Wilson made an appearance on television that he would never live down, explaining how 'Devaluation does not mean that the pound here in Britain, in your pocket or purse or in your bank, has been devalued.' In the 1964 election campaign, Wilson had claimed superior economic expertise over Tory toffs such as Alec Douglas Home, who did his sums with matchsticks. For Wilson and Chancellor Callaghan, this moment was a humiliating climb-down and a blow to their credibility.

ON THE WATERFRONT
Jack Dash, the unofficial London dockers' leader, addressing a crowd during the strike in November 1967. Dash, a communist since 1936, took pride in having been involved in every dock strike since 1945. Communists were at the time banned from taking office in the Transport and General Workers Union, hence his unofficial status. Labour relations in Britain's docks were troubled throughout the 1960s, with strikes over pay and working conditions. No doubt this hastened the closure of many port facilities, but lack of investment, foreign competition and especially the increasing use of container ships needing deep-water berths made the death of many docks inevitable. Dash saw it coming. 'Being realistic, that had to happen, and the battle was to ensure workers got a share of progress and change.' He denied that the militancy of workers had brought about the closures. 'Yes, I've been accused of shutting the docks, but in fact none of the docks closed until after I had left the industry. It was changes in trade that made them close.' He went on to write an autobiography (*Good Morning Brothers!*), and to a new job as a London tour guide. He also became a champion of pensioners' rights.

NOTICE
OOT & MOUTH
PRECAUTION
KEEP OUT

FASHION MATTERS

After the grey days of the early Sixties, there came a Technicolor explosion of creativity and exuberance, and shopping was at the heart of it. In run-down Soho, Carnaby Street was suddenly transformed into a riot of colourful boutiques selling all that was trendy and much that was tat. Here was Lord John and, later, Lady Jane, Take Six and I Was Lord Kitchener's Valet, an offshoot of the original in Portobello. Over on Chelsea's King's Road, the antique shops and Mary Quant's Bazaar were joined by Top Gear, Granny Takes a Trip and the popular Chelsea Kitchen.

To wear the daring short skirts of the Sixties, it was best to be slim – like these two young women (left), who epitomise the youthful mid-1960s look. Designer Mary Quant did more than anyone to popularise the 'Chelsea look' of short skirts and clean lines. Here (right), she has her hair styled by fellow fashion icon, Vidal Sassoon, who created her sharp, geometric, five-point cut. Warsaw-born designer Barbara Hulanicki (above) was the talent behind the hugely influential Biba. She started Biba's Postal Boutique at the urging of her husband, Stephen FitzSimon, selling long evening skirts through the _Daily Express_, but after designing a pink gingham dress for a readers' offer in the _Daily Mirror_, which sold for 25 shillings (£1.25), she moved on to a bricks-and-mortar outlet and bigger things. Her palate was subdued – shades of chestnut, plum, prune, dusky pinks. They were, she would later write, 'the dull, sad, auntie colours I had despised in my young days. They looked better in England's grey light, almost vibrant.' Princess Anne was among her customers.

'A woman is as young as her knees.'

Mary Quant

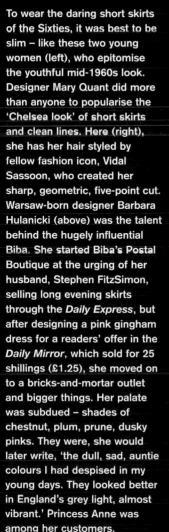

THE NEW MEN

They may not look very stylish now, but in the early Sixties the Small Faces were the height of mod chic for men (left). Men's fashions would become more hippyish as the decade wore on, ending with long hair and flared loon trousers.

Ossie Clarke (bottom left) was a seminal figure of Sixties fashion. Collaborating with his former fellow student and future wife, the textile designer Celia Birtwell, he produced a collection for the boutique Quorum in 1966.

Photographer David Bailey tries to convey to his model – Jean Shrimpton – the look he is aiming to achieve (right). Surely the best-known of the Sixties photographers, Bailey was a working-class boy from the East End of London who got into photography after finishing his National Service. In 1959 he got a job with the *Daily Express* as assistant to the photographer John French. He left to set up his own studio and secured a contract with *Vogue*. He had a fresh, innovative, irreverent style, and with his minimalist approach and use of high contrast he was breaking new ground. He helped to make stars of a rising generation of models, including Jean Shrimpton, of whom he said: 'In a way she was the cheapest model in the world – you only needed to shoot half a roll of film and then you had it … she was just a natural.' Of his own work he would say: 'I've always tried to do pictures that don't date. I always go for simplicity.'

'I never cared for fashion much, amusing little
seams and witty little pleats. It was the girls I liked.'

5010-24

SIXTIES GIRLS

Fashion model Jean Shrimpton (left) poses in a floral, op-art print mini dress and thong sandals for a promotional portrait for *Privilege*, a film by director Peter Watkins. In fairly typical Sixties style, the film had a mixed amateur and professional cast that included Shrimpton and pop singer Paul Jones, whose performances were critically panned. A graduate of the Lucie Clayton modelling school, Shrimpton was in great demand from glossy magazines on both sides of the Atlantic by the time she was 18. She fell for fashion photographer David Bailey, who was married at the time. They set up home in London, creating a menagerie that included finches and two love birds. She later had an affair with the film actor Terence Stamp.

The most famous Sixties model of them all was Twiggy – real name Lesley Hornby, from Neasden in north London.

She was just 16 and still a schoolgirl when she launched her modelling career. She wore a size six and was the very embodiment of Mary Quant's vision of the dolly-bird look: 'childishly young, naïve, unsophisticated'. Here (above), Twiggy models a see-through plastic dress in the summer of 1966. Many fashion designers experimented with adventurous materials in the Sixties, from PVC to paper.

Pop singer Sandie Shaw opened her own London boutique in September 1967. Here she is (top right), barefoot as she always appeared on stage, drawing a crowd of curious onlookers and proving that modelling is not as easy as it looks.

Hung On You was a popular boutique in Cale Street, Chelsea. By 1967, when this fashionable young woman was photographed there, skirts had reached truly miniscule proportions.

DISILLUSION SETS IN

If Swinging London was now at its height, the only way was down, and by the end of 1967 a mood of cynicism was creeping in. The ongoing party atmosphere appeared frivolous and misplaced to many commentators, bemoaning a decadent nation in terminal decline. Yet 1968 began on a high note, with a mass outbreak of patriotism that briefly confounded the pessimists. The 'I'm Backing Britain' euphoria would be short-lived, but in the months of campaigning and protest that were to follow, there was a genuine conviction that ordinary people could make a difference

TROUBLES AHEAD Two Belfast children, photographed in August 1969, seem unfazed by the soldier and barricade across the street behind them. But sectarian violence and strife will blight their growing-up years.

I'M BACKING BRITAIN

In the first week of January, 1968, five typists at Colt Heating and Ventilation Ltd in Surbiton, Surrey, decided to work an extra half-hour a day. Christine French, Brenda Mumford, Valerie White, Joan Southwell and Carolann Fry were sincere if naïve in their intentions, and had they not had to give so many interviews to the media, they might have got some typing done in their unpaid overtime. 'It was a big, terrifying fuss,' Carolann would later recall. 'We got mixed up when asked horrid questions about trade unions.' Clearly none of these young women was prepared for the furore that followed their well-meaning action, as the I'm Backing Britain campaign started to roll.

> ## 'Going to lunch at the House of Commons was lovely, but we saw all those MPs lying around with their legs up. That George Brown, with his flesh-coloured socks!'
>
> Carolann Fry, one of the typists who inspired the 'I'm Backing Britain' movement

Others rushed to emulate them. It seemed that there could be no gesture too quixotic. Author Russell Braddon waived his fee for appearing on the Simon Dee Show. Twelve Ipswich mothers gave up their free milk vouchers. A trainee accountant sent £5 to BEA towards the cost of Concorde. An army officer gave up a week's leave to assemble skates for export. A secondary school headmaster let it be known that he would not be taking 90 pupils to the Continent that summer. Dame Edith Evans resolved to bottle British fruit. And the Governor of Tasmania sent a telegram to say that all Tasmanians were 'thrilled at the finest action since the Battle of Britain'.

Not everybody was so impressed. One Scottish trade unionist described the decision to work overtime for nothing as 'stark, staring mad'. Clive Jenkins, the transport union leader, thought he perceived a capitalist plot. Tories Enoch Powell and Quintin Hogg dismissed the whole affair as a gimmick. The right-wing Powell suggested it would be better named 'Help Brainwash Britain', remarking that it was 'not only ineffably silly, but positively dangerous'. As if to prove their point, the Beyond the Fringe wig company furnished the Colt girls with Union Jack wigs, while Pye Records jumped on the bandwagon releasing a single called 'I'm Backing Britain', hastily penned by Tony Hatch and Jackie Trent and sung by Bruce Forsyth. The song ran:

'I'm backing Britain.
We're all Backing Britain.
The feeling is growing
So let's keep it going.
The good times are blowing our way.'

PATRIOTIC FERVOUR

For the first six weeks of 1968, the 'I'm Backing Britain' campaign was everywhere. The Union Jack suddenly appeared on anything and everything, from a special issue of coffee mugs rushed out by Staffordshire Potteries to T-shirts – sadly not, in the spirit of the campaign, produced in Britain, but in Portugal. This picture (left) was taken in early January to help publicise the movement. Somehow the campaign, which had begun spontaneously in the small typing pool of a Surbiton heating firm, caught a mood of defiant optimism in the face of sterling's devaluation. One man saw an opportunity. Robert Maxwell – shown below in a photograph with Rupert Murdoch in January 1969 – was the Labour MP for Buckingham and he seized on the campaign to raise his own profile. He persuaded broadcaster David Frost to invite him onto his chat show and donate £1,000 to his 'Buy British' campaign. With letters of support from well-known personalities, Maxwell took out press ads urging readers to 'act on just six … uncranky suggestions'. In February he switched his slogan to 'Sell British, Help Britain, Help Yourself'. But by March, 'I'm Backing Britain' was fizzling out and Maxwell dropped the whole enterprise. He lost his seat in 1970 and from then on concentrated on his business activities, in which he would remember the last third of his maxim, helping himself from the pension pot of his Mirror Group workers.

On 8 January, the Department of Economic Affairs enjoined the existing Industrial Society to orchestrate the campaign, and so the Society went to work to define the ways in which Britons could best help their country. Harold Wilson officially endorsed the campaign. But opposition quickly grew – perhaps because of the government backing, certainly because trade unions saw any exhortation to work unpaid overtime as a threat to their members' interests, but also because the public could see that it was ineffective and, well, a bit silly. Within a couple of months the campaign was running out of steam, and it was officially closed by autumn.

PROTEST AND UNREST

An unlooked-for consequence of the increase in the student population was a rise in angry protests by politicised youth. In January 1967, Walter Adams, the former principal of Rhodesia's University College, was appointed director of the London School of Economics. LSE Students saw Adams as having been complicit in apartheid in Ian Smith's white-ruled country. They began a 'Stop Adams' campaign, staging strikes, sit-ins and marches.

Over the next two years, student activism flared around the country. In May 1968, some 200 students occupied the administrative wing of Hull University. At Hornsey Art College in London a highly creative sit-in began that would last until 8 July, with students running the entire show from switchboard to canteen and even redecorating parts of the building.

Anti-Vietnam protests

Students and young people generally were a strong presence on two marches to protest against American involvement in Vietnam. The first demonstration, on 17 March, 1968, saw 25,000 people gathered in Trafalgar Square, where they were addressed by a charismatic young Pakistani Trotskyite, Tariq Ali, and the actress Vanessa Redgrave of the Workers' Revolutionary Party. As they made their way to the American Embassy in Grosvenor Square, the marchers chanted 'Ho, Ho, Ho Chi Minh!' in support of the North Vietnamese president. The Vietnamese Solidarity Campaign, organisers of the day's action, had a stated commitment to 'victory' for North Vietnam, which cast some doubt upon their claim that this was a 'peace march'.

When they reached Grosvenor Square there was mayhem, as mounted police with batons charged into the demonstrators. The policing was heavy-handed, although certainly some demonstrators were provocative and by today's standards the police were ill equipped to deal with the situation.

Such scenes were not confined to Britain. Throughout the summer of 1968, around the Western world, there were bloody scenes of protest and unrest. In May riots on the streets of Paris rocked de Gaulle's government. When a second London anti-Vietnam march was planned for 27 October, there were fears of a

THIN BLUE LINE

A line of uniformed police, with mounted police in back-up behind, endeavour to contain demonstrators in London's Grosvenor Square, home to the American Embassy, where they are protesting against the Vietnam War in March 1968. Some of the police saw their role as protective, warning the marchers that if they attempted to storm the embassy they risked being shot. A truncheon blow or a few hours in a police cell were more likely. Anti-war passions ran high in Britain, fuelled by hard-hitting coverage of the carnage by such great photographers as Don McCullin. But cynics commented that, since Britain was not involved in the fighting and young British men would not be called up to serve in Vietnam, it was an easy gesture to turn up for the demo – and to go home feeling good about yourself.

WOMEN AGAINST THE WAR

More than 400 women gathered in protest outside the American Embassy in Grosvenor Square in February 1968, then set off to Downing Street brandishing placards (left). By June 1966, after US bombers attacked the north Vietnamese cities of Hanoi and Haiphong, only one in three Britons expressed support for the war and half thought that America should withdraw. Harold Wilson, under pressure, expressed his 'regret' at aggressive military actions. With some skill he managed to maintain friendly relations with the USA, while steadfastly refusing to send British troops to war. One of the most prominent women in the protest against the war was the actress Vanessa Redgrave, seen here (below) addressing an anti-Vietnam rally outside the American Embassy in March 1968. Her white paper headband is a traditional Vietnamese symbol of mourning. With her is activist Tariq Ali (centre). After one such rally, Ali recounted how the marchers poured down Park Lane to take 'the next best symbol of American imperialism' – the Hilton Hotel. Some of the protesters then urged that they storm the Playboy Club, but the action was vetoed when it was recalled that Hugh Hefner, American owner of the club and of *Playboy* magazine, had taken a stand against the war.

pitched battle. Students streamed out of the LSE chanting, 'London, Paris, Rome, Berlin, we shall fight and we shall win'. In the event, they did not fight – and they did not win. The event passed off peacefully, with a crowd of 30,000 gathering in Hyde Park to listen to speeches. Some 5,000 mustered in Grosvenor Square. There were a very few arrests. The press consensus the next day was that the British police were wonderful.

January 1969 found the LSE students up in arms once more against Walter Adams. They took sledgehammers to specially erected iron gates, they boycotted lectures and occupied the student common room. Then, somehow, hostilities died down almost as quickly as they had arisen – although not in Vietnam, where war would continue until 1975.

Race relations

On 20 April, 1968, in the Midland Hotel in Birmingham, Enoch Powell, the Conservative MP for Wolverhampton Southwest, made an inflammatory speech against the government's proposed Race Relations Bill. He lamented that to witness the inflow of immigrants was 'like watching a nation busily engaged in

CONTRADICTORY RHETORIC
Following his infamous 'rivers of blood' speech, Tory MP Enoch Powell was branded a racist and the judgment has stuck. But the reality of Powell was more complicated. In 1959, for example, he roundly criticised British treatment of the Mau-Mau in Kenya. Born in Birmingham, the son of a schoolteacher, he took a double starred first in Classics at Cambridge. He rose from private to brigadier in the British army during the war and was awarded an OBE for his services. As the Empire crumbled, he believed Britain should stop trying to be a world power. He advocated forming a defence alliance with Western Europe – but opposed joining the EEC. His controversial, often seemingly contradictory views stemmed from deeply held convictions and the cold application of logic. He turned down an invitation to stand for the National Front.

heaping its own funeral pyre'. In his concluding phrases, he warned ominously: 'As I look ahead, I am filled with foreboding. Like the Roman, I seem to see "the River Tiber foaming with much blood".'

Powell was immediately sacked from the shadow cabinet by Tory leader Edward Heath, and he was reviled for the speech up and down the land. But he had struck a chord with a section of the public. He received thousands of letters of support from people who shared his concerns about the loss of national identity, or about competition from immigrants for jobs and houses. People marched for Powell; people marched against him. He required police protection.

In the background to Powell's speech had been the arrival in Britain, throughout 1967, of around 1,000 Asians each month from newly independent Kenya, where discriminatory legislation brought in by President Jomo Kenyatta had made life impossible for them. By 1968 the influx had risen to 2,000 a month, making newspaper headlines. TV news screens were filled with images of weary would-be migrants queuing for British passports or to board planes. Powell predicted that a million African-Asians would eventually arrive.

Whether or not the Labour government believed such predictions, it felt pressure to respond. In February 1968, with James Callaghan now Home Secretary, the Commonwealth Immigrants Act was rushed through Parliament, slamming the door on all but a few Kenyan Asians – although a clause still allowed the entry of white Kenyans. This was controversial law-making, which caused deep affront in Labour ranks. 'That a Socialist government should be responsible fills me with shame and despair', said MP Ben Whitaker.

If Callaghan's aim with the Commonwealth Immigrants Act had been to appease racist sentiments by restricting immigration, another proposal put before Parliament the following month was aimed at strengthening anti-discrimination laws to protect immigrants already in Britain. Since 1965 it had been illegal to discriminate on grounds of colour or race in public places. Now, it was proposed

LIVING WITH DISCRIMINATION

A man walks by graffiti calling for his would-be nemesis, Enoch Powell, to be installed in No 10 Downing Street. Racial relations improved towards the end of the decade, but equality was a distant dream. Discrimination was a fact of everyday life for Commonwealth immigrants, whose experience of the 'Mother Country' was often bitterly disillusioning. Whatever their skills, they were restricted to low-paid, low-status jobs – or excluded altogether. Pubs and restaurants quite openly banned 'blacks' until the first Race Relations Act, passed in 1965, made such discrimination illegal. The Act of 1968 extended this to make it illegal to refuse housing or employment on grounds of colour or race.

to extend anti-discrimination laws to cover housing, employment and public services. Powell's 'rivers of blood' speech was aimed as a broadside against this extension of the race Relations Act and his rhetoric was deliberately designed to stir up public feeling against it. He made reference to 'the black man having the whip hand', to a once-quiet street now 'a place of noise and confusion', to excrement being pushed through her letterbox of an elderly white woman who had refused to rent rooms to non-whites and was being tailed by 'charming, wide-grinning piccaninnies chanting "Racialist"'. It was sustained, cold-blooded incitement to race hatred – and Powell knew it. Before making the speech he had told a friend, the editor of the *Wolverhampton Express and Star*: 'I'm going to make a speech at the weekend and it's going to go up, fizz, like a rocket; but whereas all rockets fall to earth, this one is going to stay up.'

Powell was wrong. His rocket fell like every other and the rivers never did run red with blood. Had they done so, as Bernard Levin commented, Powell would have been as responsible as any man. The Race Relations Act came into force in November 1968. It was not a magic solution to discrimination, but it was a step on the way to a fairer, multi-ethnic society in Britain.

SEEKING A NEW HOME
Bone weary and clutching a few possessions, Asian immigrants arrive at London Airport on 24 February, 1968. They had been forced to flee Kenya by the new, independent Kenyan government's discriminatory policies. As Commonwealth citizens, they had the right to come to Britain and the exodus saw some 1,000 Asians a month arrive by plane throughout 1967, rising to 2,000 a month in 1968.

In place of strife

Meanwhile, inflation was rising and strikes – most of them unofficial – were taking a toll on the economy. In 1968, some 4.7 million days were lost to industrial action. There were sit-ins and go-slows. Harold Wilson's 'beer and sandwiches' diplomacy was clearly not winning over the union leaders.

Wilson appointed Barbara Castle as his Secretary of State for Employment in 1968, following her successes as Transport Minister. She came up with a classic piece of wishful thinking, which she put foward in 1969 in a white paper entitled 'In Place of Strife'. She had named the document in homage to her hero, Aneurin Bevan, who had written a book called *In Place of Fear*. Castle proposed new powers for government to order pre-strike ballots and impose settlements on unofficial strikes and inter-union disputes. It called for a 28-day cooling-off period before any strike action. Those who broke the rules would be fined.

Castle's blueprint faced opposition within both Cabinet and the Parliamentary Labour Party, and was roundly rejected by the unions. At a dinner that summer at Chequers, the Prime Minister's official country residence, Hugh Scanlon – general secretary of the Transport and General Workers' Union – warned that the new legislation was not acceptable. Wilson and Castle went so far as to consider resignation. Instead, 'In Place of Strife' was quietly dropped, but the mishandling of the affair resulted in humiliation for Wilson.

THE RED QUEEN

Barbara Castle, seen here in 1966, was a clever, single-minded, pragmatic woman, a committed champion of ethical socialism whose mission was 'to inch people towards a more civilised society'. Her nickname, 'the Red Queen', was both for her firebrand speeches and her red hair. She was not herself a driver, and was not initially thrilled to be given the Transport Minister's job by Harold Wilson in 1965, but she rose to the challenge. Her Road Safety Act of 1966 introduced the breathalyser, which earned her widespread unpopularity. Other unpopular measures in the Act were the imposition of a top speed limit of 70mph and legislation towards compulsory seatbelts. At the time, she received hate mail – even death threats – but she persevered, undeterred, and made a considerable contribution to road safety.

BLOWING IN THE BAG

A motorist suspected of driving under the influence of drink is required to blow into a breathalyser (below), a deterrent that first came into operation on 9 October, 1967. The Transport Minister, Barbara Castle, faced opposition not just from motorists but from the drinks industry. She was accused of undermining civil liberties, to which she replied that she did not recognise anybody's civil right to kill someone because they were drunk. Her attitude was vindicated: in the first year there were 1,152 fewer road deaths and 11,177 fewer serious injuries. Before the imposition of the breathalyser, magistrates had tended to be lenient with drink drivers, perhaps thinking, 'There but for the grace of God go I.' Now a legal sanction was imposed by Parliament from above: a positive breath test would incur a year's ban from driving.

CRIME AND PUNISHMENT

On 5 March, 1969, two vicious criminals were finally sentenced to life imprisonment. The Kray twins, Reginald and Ronald, might have hanged had the death penalty not been suspended, to be finally abolished on 18 December.

'Reggie and Ronnie' were sadistic London gangland killers who, as nightclub owners, enjoyed a perverse kind of celebrity. They consorted with actors, starlets, boxers, even MPs, and posed for photographer David Bailey, who found them exciting. They stood trial at the Old Bailey, with accomplices including their older brother Charlie, for the murder of Jack 'The Hat' McVitie, who had been repeatedly stabbed by Reggie in a London flat, while Ronnie held him down. Ronnie Kray was also found guilty of shooting dead George Cornell in 1966, in the Blind Beggar pub on the Mile End Road, as the Walker Brothers' hit 'The Sun Ain't Gonna Shine Any More' played on the jukebox. Cornell, an associate of the rival Richardson gang, had called Ronnie a 'fat poof'.

For the twins, 'life' was to mean just that – or very nearly. Ronald would die, aged 61, in hospital after collapsing of a massive heart attack in Broadmoor. Reginald died aged 66, of bladder cancer, in the honeymoon suite at the Beefeater Town House Hotel in Norwich, Norfolk, having been freed on compassionate grounds in the terminal stages of disease by Home Secretary Jack Straw.

Grades of murder

Thanks perhaps to their connections, which gave them a spurious aura of glamour, the Krays did not attract great public odium. Apologists for the twins say that they killed only their gangland rivals. The feeling was that fellow criminals were fair game. Children are not fair game, and there were prominent, aberrant crimes in the 1960s that aroused utter public revulsion.

The so-called 'Moors Murderers', Ian Brady and Myra Hindley, were put on trial in April 1966 for the murders of 10-year-old Lesley Ann Downey, 12-year-old John Kilbride and 17-year-old Edward Evans. The jury at Chester Assizes were sickened to hear tapes of the torture of Lesley Ann, while Christmas music played in the background. None could ever again listen to 'The Little Drummer Boy', by Ray Conniff and his singers. While the little girl was heard to plead with her tormentors, women in the court covered their ears; one wept. John Stalker, a detective sergeant with Greater Manchester police, later said of the case: 'Nothing in criminal behaviour before or since has penetrated my heart with quite the same paralysing intensity.'

On 7 May, 1966, Brady was convicted of all three murders and given three life sentences. Hindley received two life sentences, with an additional seven years for harbouring Brady; she was acquitted of the murder of John Kilbride. Two decades later, Hindley and Brady would confess to the murders of 16-year-old Pauline Reade and 12-year-old Keith Bennett. Pauline Reade's body was found on Saddleworth Moor in 1987.

THE TERRIBLE TWINS

East End gangsters the Kray twins, Reggie (left) and Ronnie, refresh themselves with a nice cup of Rosie Lee after 36 hours of questioning by police over the murder of George Cornell in 1966. The criminal activities of the Krays and their rivals the Richardsons were well known to the police, but such was their reign of terror in East London that witnesses dared not testify against them. The Krays attracted many celebrity hangers-on, and intellectuals who should have known better were openly in thrall. The photographer David Bailey declared that he 'liked them', while the *Sunday Times* journalist Francis Wyndham went way over the top. In a caption to a Bailey portrait of all three Krays – Reggie, Ronnie and their elder brother Charlie – Wyndham wrote that to be with them was 'to enter the atmosphere (laconic, lavish, dangerous) of an early Bogart movie where life is reduced to its simplest terms yet remains ambiguous'. The evil that men do lives after them – and so does their mystique. To this day, these vicious murderers remain a source of fascination.

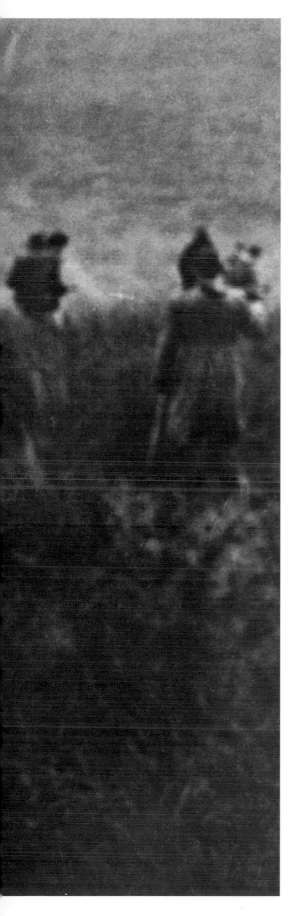

A MOTHER'S WORST NIGHTMARE
Mrs Ann Downey (left) watches police searchers on Saddleworth Moor in Lancashire, where the body of her daughter, 10-year-old Lesley Ann, was found. At a 15-day trial of Myra Hindley and Ian Brady (below) at Chester Assizes, the jury had to hear tapes of Lesley Ann pleading for her life and to see pornographic pictures of her. Mrs Downey was not spared; she was asked to identify her child's voice and to confirm that it was she in the picture, naked, gagged, bound to a chair. Ann Downey pledged that if Hindley were ever freed, she would personally kill her. Until her death from cancer in February 1999, Ann West (as she became) campaigned against any form of parole for Hindley. In her dying days she swore that she would haunt her from beyond the grave. She had an unlikely ally in Brady, who, from high-security Ashworth Hospital, accused Hindley of the murder of Lesley Ann. He charged that she was 'a manipulative liar'. 'The most hated woman in Britain', Hindley died in hospital of respiratory failure on 15 November, 2002. Brady is still incarcerated

 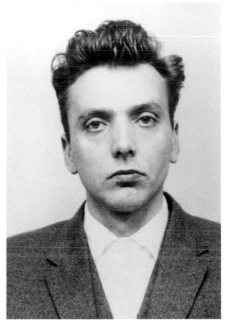

In its own way more disturbing was the case of Mary Bell, aged 11, sentenced to life detention in December 1968, for the manslaughter by strangling of two boys, aged three and four, 'solely for the pleasure and excitement of killing'.

In this context it is just possible to see how the Great Train Robbers might have been regarded as lovable rogues, the Krays as 'diamond geezers'.

TIMES OF TROUBLE

In the late afternoon of 14 August, 1969, following three nights of violence, 300 troops from the 1st Battalion of the Prince of Wales's Own Regiment of Yorkshire occupied the centre of Londonderry, Northern Ireland, relieving the exhausted Royal Ulster Constabulary (RUC) and the part-time pro-Protestant 'B Specials'. This signalled the start of a new phase in the historic struggle between the two-thirds-majority Protestant population, descendants of Scottish and English settlers,

With bombs a very real and constant threat, a woman in Belfast submits to a roadside search of her shopping by British soldiers in 1969 (left). The residents of Northern Ireland would have to get used to such inconveniences in the years ahead, as well as the depressing presence of barbed wire and checkpoints, as armed forces struggled to contain the mounting violence.

who were fiercely proud to be British, and the politically marginalised Roman Catholics, who since partition in 1921 had yearned to be part of an independent Ireland. Endemic inequality compounded the alienation. Discrimination against Catholics was manifest in employment and housing. Not only were Catholics outnumbered two to one, but local government electoral boundaries were drawn to favour the Ulster Unionists, even in predominantly Catholic areas. Only rate-payers were eligible to vote in local elections, which disproportionately reduced the number of Catholics eligible.

By 1966, there had been outbreaks of rioting. Three priests were murdered by the Ulster Volunteer Force, which was at once banned by Northern Ireland Prime Minister Terence O'Neill. Peaceful marches in October 1968 turned ugly when the RUC resorted to strong-arm tactics to disperse the Catholic protesters. O'Neill was called to Whitehall for urgent talks, after which he introduced some reforms, including fairer allocation of social housing. But with many grievances unresolved, and the continued denial of one-man-one-vote, civil rights marches went on.

In what he termed a 'crossroads election', O'Neill went to the people of Ulster in February 1969, seeking a mandate for change. He was returned to power but

TROUBLES ONCE MORE
In August 1969, 'The Battle of the Bogside' broke out in the city of Derry (Londonderry to Unionists) after the RUC attempted to disperse a Nationalist crowd protesting against the Apprentice Boys' march along the city wall. After three days of rioting, the British army was called in to restore order. The riot was one of the first major conflicts in 'The Troubles', and sparked a series of others. The picture below shows heavily armed police in Derry on 17 August, after a petrol bomb explosion during a civil rights march. In Belfast, streets were torched and more than 3,500 – mainly Catholic – families were driven from their homes.

with a slim majority, and resigned two months later. His successor, Major James Chichester-Clark, resolved to push ahead with reforms. Meanwhile, demonstrations were becoming more confrontational. Paramilitary groups were marshalling on both sides of the divide.

In July began the marching season for the Orange Order – Northern Ireland's largest Protestant organisation, dating from the 17th century when William of Orange led the fight to defeat Catholic James II at the Battle of the Boyne. Men wearing bowler hats and orange sashes paraded banners proclaiming the victory. This was followed in August by the annual Apprentice Boys' march in Londonderry (Derry) celebrating 'the shutting of the gates', when 13 young apprentices closed the city gates to hold off King James's army at the start of a 105-day siege. When this descended into skirmishing – in what would be known as 'The Battle of the Bogside' – the first contingent of 300 British troops was

deployed, at the request of Chichester-Clark. It was to be, according to the British government, a 'limited operation' and the troops would be pulled out within days.

In the event, 'Operation Banner' was to last 38 years, the British army's longest continuous military operation. Over that time it would involve 300,000 military personnel, of whom 763 were killed by paramilitaries, before responsibility for security in Northern Ireland was passed back to the police at midnight on 31 July, 2007. Even then, a garrison of 5,000 troops remained in support.

END OF THE ROAD

In 1962, John Lennon had married Cynthia Powell, whom he had met at art school. Their son, Julian, was born in 1963. The couple divorced in 1968, and on 20 March, 1969, Lennon married his lover, Japanese conceptual artist Yoko Ono, by special licence in a three-minute ceremony in Gibraltar. The bride wore a white crêpe mini dress, the groom a hairy jacket; both wore white tennis shoes.

For a week, on their honeymoon at the Amsterdam Hilton, the couple staged a 'Bed-in for Peace', inviting the press into their hotel room and talking about their decision to make this protest against the Vietnam War. Signs on the walls read 'Bed Peace', 'Hair Peace', 'Stay in Bed' and 'Grow Your Hair'. If everyone stayed in bed and grew their hair, ran the impeccable logic, there would be no more war.

It was a memorable stunt and the couple got a lot of publicity, but Lennon also came in for much media derision. Not surprisingly, they failed to persuade US President Richard Nixon to reconsider his foreign policy – or grow his hair.

Division in the Beatles

Yoko Ono was already something of a hate figure, demonised for destroying the Beatles, as relationships within the group became strained. To be fair, this was not all her doing. There was already acrimony between Lennon and McCartney, who at the height of their collaboration had been one of the most felicitous songwriter partnerships of all time. Wealth and fame had changed them. They were no longer a happy or cohesive group. Yoko merely put the lid on it. As soon as he met her, Lennon would admit, 'that was the end of the boys'.

He later told the editor of *Rolling Stone* magazine, 'One of the main reasons the Beatles ended is because ... we got fed up with being sidemen for Paul. After Brian [Epstein] died, we collapsed. Paul took over and supposedly led us. But what is leading us when we went round in circles? Paul had the impression we should be

'It seemed that I either had to be married to them or Yoko. I chose Yoko ...'

John Lennon, on the split with the Beatles

THE NEWLYWEDS
It would not have been everyone's idea of a honeymoon. After John Lennon and his new wife, Yoko Ono, married on 20 March, 1969, they took to their bed in the Presidential Suite at the Amsterdam Hilton, and invited the world's press and broadcast media to join them every day from 9am to 9pm. They spent seven days thus, in protest against the Vietnam War in particular, and violence in the world in general. Anyone hoping for some kind of sexual exposure would have been disappointed. The couple were decorously covered up in old-fashioned pyjamas, behaving, as John said, 'like angels'. During April the couple sent acorns to presidents and other heads of state around the world, expressing the hope that they might plant them as symbols of peace. Tall oaks from little acorns grow but none, as far as we know, grew from this initiative. On 25 November, 1969, as part of his continuing peace protest with Yoko, John Lennon handed back his MBE.

LEFT BEHIND
On the sweltering afternoon of 5 July, 1969, at a free concert in Hyde Park, Mick Jagger addressed crowds numbering 250,000, to honour former Rolling Stone Brian Jones. Jagger recited from *Adonais*, Shelley's elegy on the death of Keats: 'Peace, peace! He is not dead, he doth not sleep.' When he had read his tribute, thousands of white butterflies were released into the air, and the concert got underway with Mick Taylor – shown on stage with Jagger (above right) – on lead guitar. Many in the crowd remained subdued, but a few got up to dance (right). Brian Jones – seen above in a photograph from 1968 – had drowned three days before in the swimming-pool at his Sussex farmhouse, Cotchford Farm, once home to Winnie the Pooh's creator, A A Milne. His 'sacking' from the band by Jagger and Keith Richards the previous month led some to suspect suicide, but the coroner found that he had died by 'misadventure' as a result of drug and alcohol abuse. He was the first of the so-called '27 Club' – musicians of the 1960s and 70s who died at the age of 27. Before long he would be joined by Jimi Hendrix, Janis Joplin and Jim Morrison of The Doors.

thankful for what he did, for keeping the Beatles going. But he kept it going for his own sake.' Lennon had, he said, felt forced to choose between Yoko and the band.

Ultimately, there was no one individual to blame. The Beatles' story had run its course, as, by now, had so much that was quintessentially Sixties. 'Things fall apart; the centre cannot hold.' In 1970, the Beatles would finally disband.

It's only rock'n'roll
One band that did keep going come what may was the Rolling Stones. In early June 1969 they fired founder member, lead guitarist Brian Jones, whose excessive and casual consumption of alcohol and drugs had made him a liability. They planned to stage a free open-air concert in Hyde Park that July to introduce new guitarist, Mick Taylor. Three days before the concert, Jones was found dead at his Sussex home. The Stones rolled on, turning the concert into a wake.

THAT'S ENTERTAINMENT

The decade saw radical changes in every field of entertainment – in music, theatre, cinema, radio and particularly in television, where developments in technology were as dramatic as those in presentational style and content. In January 1960 the choice for viewers was between the worthy BBC with its Reithian aims to educate, inform and entertain, and the ITV network of a dozen or so regional companies,

which had more freedom to appeal to the mass market. All broadcasts were in black and white. TV sets had tiny screens, needed several minutes to warm up and were prone to breakdown – when a good thump did not restore the picture, the repairman would be called in with his bag of spare parts.

Television comes of age

In 1962, the American satellite Telstar made possible instant feedback between continents. A third channel, the highbrow BBC2, was launched on 20 April, 1964. It got off to an inauspicious start, when a power cut blacked out BBC Television Centre. BBC2 was broadcast on 625 lines, making for sharper pictures, although a new TV set and aerial were required to get the channel and see the benefit of the improved quality. The 625 system made colour television possible, which duly began on 1 July, 1967, with an outside broadcast of tennis at Wimbledon. Colour remained a luxury that few could afford – by the end of 1969, there were just 200,000 sets in the whole of the UK.

A high spot of the week was ITV's variety show 'Sunday Night at the London Palladium'. 'Songs of Praise', a simple programme of uplifting hymn-singing, was an instant success. Launched by the BBC in 1961, it is still with us nearly half a century later. Another programme that has stood the test of time is ITV's breakthrough soap opera, 'Coronation Street'. Set in a fictitious working-class suburb of Manchester, it was a dramatic departure from the clipped 'Queen's English' that dominated the BBC, and was an immediate hit with the public.

'Mondays and Wednesdays, I live for them … half past seven tonight and I shall be in Paradise!'

Sir John Betjeman, Poet Laureate, on 'Coronation Street'

THE STREET
December 1960 saw the launch by Granada of its enduringly successful soap opera 'Coronation Street'. From the start its great strength was its characters – brilliantly conceived, written and acted – and the everyday drama of their lives. One of the originals was Ena Sharples (above), with her hatchet face and hairnet, played by Violet Carson. She spent her free time in the Snug Bar of the Rover's Return, with her friends Minnie Caldwell and Martha Longhurst, putting the world to rights over a glass of stout. Another gem was Hilda Ogden (top), played by Jean Alexander from 1964 to 1987. On the death of her screen husband, Stan, in 1985 (following the real-life death of the actor Bernard Youens) she was deluged with condolence cards.

The BBC responded with its own more gritty dramas. 'Z Cars', which first aired in 1962, brought a new edge to police drama. It was located in Newtown, an overspill estate in Liverpool's docklands, a world away from Dock Green, where the avuncular PC George Dixon trod the beat. The central characters of 'Z Cars' were variously flawed. Violence might be met with violence. The BBC received complaints from the public, from the Police Federation, and from Dixon actor Jack Warner, but most people liked it. Within a few weeks 'Z Cars' had an audience of 14 million, drawn to the portrayal of a less idealised world.

'Doctor Who' began in 1963, filling the Saturday teatime slot between the popular sports programme 'Grandstand' and the pop music 'Juke Box Jury'. It would become the longest-running sci-fi serial in TV history. The Doctor, aged 720, hailed from the planet Gallifre, and traversed both time and space in a faulty machine known as the TARDIS (Time and Relative Dimensions in Space) in the shape of a blue police box – a familiar piece of street furniture at the time. From behind the nation's sofas children watched bug-eyed and open-mouthed, as the evil Daleks screamed 'Exterminate! Exterminate!'

COP CARS AND TIME TRAVEL
The first Dr Who, played by William
Hartnell, confronts some extraterrestrials
in 1964. In terms of scariness, the
slumber-suit costumes don't really stack
up against the Daleks. Famously, the
Doctor travelled in a special police
telephone box. In 'Z Cars', the BBC's new
police drama, officers drove around in
pairs in a Ford Zephyr. Here, (above right)
actors Jeremy Kemp and James Ellis – as
PCs Bob Steele and Bert Lynch – are seen
filming in the studio.

'Doctor Who' was commissioned by Canadian-born Sydney Newman, the BBC's
brilliant head of drama, responsible for hiring gifted directors and adventurous
young writers, whose plays reflected the realities of British life – what Newman
called 'agitational contemporaneity'. 'I found this country to be somewhat
class-ridden,' Newman explained with masterly understatement. 'Television
dramas were usually adaptations of stage plays, and invariably about the upper
classes. I said "Damn the upper classes, they don't even own televisions!"'

Newman began his British TV career with ABC, taking charge of the
Armchair Theatre slot. At ABC he was responsible for the creation of 'The
Avengers', one of the best-loved series of all time, which first aired in 1961. It was
a quintessentially British spy romp, starring suave Patrick Macnee as John Steed,
with Honor Blackman in leather cat suit and high boots as his female sidekick
Catherine Gale. In 1964 Gale made way for a new companion, Emma Peel, played
by Diana Rigg of the Royal Shakespeare Company.

At the BBC Newman instituted the Wednesday Play – later Play For Today –
which included such searing dramas as Jeremy Sandford's 'Cathy Come Home'

'My approach was to cater for the
people who were buying low-cost things
like soap every day. The ordinary bloke.'

Sydney Newman, head of BBC drama

MERRY BLEEDING CHRISTMAS
Mike (Tony Booth) baits his father-in-law, watched by Rita (Una Stubbs) and Else (Dandy Nichols), in a seasonal episode of 'Till Death Us Do Part'. Alf Garnett was played by Warren Mitchell, who was voted TV actor of the year for the role in 1965. Alf's swearing was legendary. Missing the point, as she often did, Mary Whitehouse expressed scepticism that anyone would use 121 'bloodies' in half an hour. The writer Johnny Speight was more disappointed that some fans of the show missed the fact that Alf was a send-up, satirising racist and right-wing views.

and Jim Allen's 'The Lump', about the exploitation of casual labour in the building trade. Complaints from Mary Whitehouse gave viewing figures a healthy boost. Not that the strand dealt only in unrelenting misery – there was mystery, romance, science fiction and comedy.

A golden age of comedy

The decade produced some superb situation comedies, which practically the whole nation would settle down to watch each week. 'Steptoe and Son', written by Ray Galton and Alan Simpson, began life as a one-off episode of Comedy Playhouse, mixing comedy and pathos in almost equal measure. The tale of rag-and-bone men ran from 1962 to 1965, with aspirational son Harold trying to break away from his 'dirty old man' father, Albert. In a curious incidence of life imitating art, the actor Harold H Corbett felt stifled and trapped by his role as Harold. Then came 'The Likely Lads', penned by Dick Clement and Ian La Frenais, which ran from 1964 to 1966. Set on Tyneside, it made a star of actor James Bolam.

'Till Death Us Do Part', which launched in 1965, was a new departure in situation comedy, tackling head-on the racial and social issues affecting working-class Britain. The writer, Johnny Speight, created a memorable monster as its central character: Alf Garnett was a foul-mouthed East End docker who fulminated against 'coons', women, the Labour party, the Common Market and much else besides. 'Shut up and listen, you might learn something,' Alf would rant from his armchair at his 'silly moo' wife, Else, his giggly daughter, Rita, and 'Scouse git' son-in-law played by Tony Booth, father of Cherie, the future Mrs Anthony Blair.

'Dad's Army' arrived on Britain's TV screens in 1968. And then something completely different happened. On 5 October, 1969, the first episode of zany, surrealistic 'Monty Python's Flying Circus' was aired to an unsuspecting public.

Realism and escapism

The BBC's 'Panorama', which had launched in 1953, was joined by Granada Television's flagship documentary series 'World In Action' in 1963. Together they beamed the troubles and preoccupations of the world into the nation's homes: the Cold War, the space race, the civil rights movement, Vietnam, the Middle East – all were covered, along with poverty, discord and scandal closer to home.

Costume dramas were hugely popular. BBC2's 1967 adaptation of John Galsworthy's *The Forsyte Saga* held watchers spellbound for 26 Sunday evenings.

BLACK AND WHITE TV
There were few black faces on TV in the 1960s, and those that were were white men in grease paint. 'The Black and White Minstrel Show', first screened by the BBC in 1958, was a Saturday night favourite, at its height attracting audiences of 18 million. Drawing upon a tradition in the music halls of a century before, it featured the George Mitchell Minstrels, with female song and dance troupes the Television Toppers and Mitchell Maids, and a variety of stand-up comedians. There was an undeniably upbeat, sing-along appeal about the shows, but they were coming to the end of their acceptability. On 18 May, 1967, the Campaign Against Racial Discrimination delivered a petition to the BBC requesting that the programme be axed. And so it was – but not until July 1978, by which time it had run its course anyway.

A DOG'S LIFE
Petra the Blue Peter dog gets down to a mountain of fan mail. Petra joined 'Blue Peter' in 1962 as a kind of shared pet for all the kids who had none. Sadly, the original Petra died after just one appearance, but her young fans never knew. She was replaced by a near-identical mutt, who gave birth to eight puppies in 1965, one of which, Patch, remained with the show. Fred the tortoise was introduced in 1963 – and renamed Freda when he turned out to be a she.

The episode in which the wealthy solicitor Soames Forsyte (Eric Porter) raped Irene (Nyree Dawn Porter), the wife who rejected him, caused genuine shock.

For children, television improved immeasurably over the decade. American imports increased choice, with lots of Westerns, Batman, Hanna Barbera cartoons – Tom and Jerry, Huckleberry Hound, Yogi Bear, The Flintstones – and Gerry Anderson's animatronic puppet spectaculars such as Stingray and Thunderbirds. 'Blue Peter', the BBC's long-running children's programme first aired in October 1958, presented by actor Christopher Trace and former Miss Great Britain, Leila Williams. Valerie Singleton became a presenter in 1962, showing children how to make just about anything from cardboard toilet-roll tubes, empty washing-up bottles and sticky-backed plastic. She was joined in 1965 by John Noakes, who would become the show's longest-serving presenter.

Stage and screen

The Sixties saw a 'second wave' of talented, innovative, mostly male playwrights taking theatre forward from the 'Angry Young Men' of the Fifties. Czech-born Tom Stoppard made his stage writing debut for the Edinburgh Fringe Festival in 1966 with *Rosencrantz and Guildenstern Are Dead*. Alan Ayckbourn developed a fine line in nuanced comedies of suburban and middle-class life. David Mercer, from Wakefield, the son of an engine driver and a domestic servant, explored themes of mental illness, class conflict and alienation. But theatre catered to the few – and the avant-garde to just a minority of that few. Most people preferred a rollicking musical, such as Lionel Bart's *Oliver!*, or a detective yarn such as Agatha Christie's *Murder on the Orient Express*.

Writers such as the outrageous, openly homosexual Joe Orton courted controversy by confronting issues of sexuality, in defiance of censorship. An

EVERGREEN MUSICALS

For all the new innovations of the Sixties, old-fashioned musicals with memorable songs continued to hold audiences enraptured. The stage production of *My Fair Lady* had starred Julie Andrews as Eliza Doolittle, the cockney flower girl, but she was replaced in the film version by Audrey Hepburn, an established Hollywood star. Hepburn is seen here (far right) alongside Rex Harrison, who kept his role as Professor Higgins (centre), and Wilfred Hyde White as Colonel Pickering (left). The score by Lerner and Loewe produced such enduring songs as 'I Could Have Danced All Night' and 'Wouldn't It Be Loverly?'. Meanwhile, the quintessentially English Julie Andrews won the starring role in *Mary Poppins*, which brought her an Oscar for Best Actress In 1964. The following year she had an even bigger hit as Maria in Robert Wise's film version of Rodgers' and Hammerstein's *The Sound of Music*. It was set against the dark background of Nazism, yet managed to be light-hearted and uplifting. Andrews is seen here (bottom) attending the Hollywood premiere of the film, with six of the seven young actors who played the Von Trapp children.

exchange of letters in the *Daily Telegraph* about his play *Entertaining Mr Sloane* epitomises the tension between radical and reactionary thinking – between those who saw gratuitous filth in his tale of bisexual hi-jinks, and those who saw art, stiff with black humour and violence. A Peter Pinnell harrumphed that the work was 'nothing more than a highly sensationalised, lurid, crude and over-dramatised picture of life at its lowest.' Mrs Edna Welthorpe concurred: 'I myself was nauseated by this endless parade of mental and physical perversion. And to be told that such a disgusting piece of filth now passes for humour! Today's young playwrights take it upon themselves to flaunt their contempt for ordinary, decent people.' A more liberal John Carlsen weighed in: 'One agrees that ordinary, decent people are the salt of the earth and the backbone of this country – but they do not make subjects for exciting, stimulating drama' – and so it went on. In fact, they were all penned by Orton himself, who was on a mission to provoke voyeuristic prudes. 'Sex is the only way to infuriate them,' he wrote in 1967, shortly before he was murdered by his lover, Kenneth Halliwell.

Orton's play had made it onto the stage only after the censor's blue pencil had struck out several expletives. But in 1968, the Theatres Act ended 231 years of the Lord Chamberlain's powers of censorship. The night after the Act came into force, the curtain went up on *Hair*, a hippy rock musical hot off Broadway, in which the whole cast stripped off at the end of the first act. The next year saw the opening of *Oh! Calcutta!*, an 'experiment in elegant erotica' by drama critic Kenneth Tynan. The title was a pun on 'O, quel cul t'as' (what a bum you have!), from a painting by Clovis Trouille. The floodgates appeared open to a stream of nudity, but those who feared a tide of filth need not have worried: it never materialised.

THE STAGE MEETS THE SIXTIES

The conservative theatregoing audiences were still drawn to the classics, to bedroom farces and detective yarns. Yet a minority were learning to expect the unexpected from playwrights such as Tom Stoppard and Harold Pinter with his dark themes in mundane settings, nuanced, ambiguous dialogue, abstractions, speaking silences and sense of underlying menace.

DRAMATIC TALENTS
The playwright Tom Stoppard in 1967, aged 29 (left). He had been born Tom Straussler in Czechoslovakia, but when he was two years old his family moved to Singapore, where his father was killed. When his mother subsequently settled in England, he took his stepfather's name. By the time this photograph was taken, Stoppard already had a body of television work under his belt – his first TV play, 'A Walk on the Water', was screened in 1963 – and he was enjoying his first major stage success in London with *Rosencrantz and Guildenstern are Dead*. The play, which retold Hamlet from the perspective of two minor Shakespeare characters, was hailed as a dramatic masterpiece.

Albert Finney, at age 24, enjoys a beer and a fag in his favourite pub behind London's Cambridge Theatre in 1961. By this time Finney was an established stage actor, but his big breakthrough came with his second film and the role of Arthur Seaton, an anarchic and disillusioned lathe operator in Karel Reisz's film version of Alan Sillitoe's landmark novel, *Saturday Night and Sunday Morning*. A number of angry-young-man roles followed for Finney, before his portrayal of Tom Jones in the eponymous 1963 film won him an Academy Award as Best Actor.

'I was the first man to be seen
sleeping with another man's wife
in an English film.'

Albert Finney on *Saturday Night and Sunday Morning*

MR OLIVER

Composer and lyricist Lionel Bart (above), pictured during rehearsals for a West End play on 6 February, 1961. Bart was one of the major songwriters for popular musicals in Britain in the late 1950s and 1960s. He is best remembered for his musical adaptation of Charles Dickens' *Oliver Twist*, which included such memorable songs as 'Food Glorious Food', 'As Long As He Needs Me' and 'Consider Yourself'. *Oliver* started its first long West End run in 1960 and notched up 2,618 performances. Following its huge success on stage, it was made into a film in 1968.

THE AGE OF AQUARIUS

The cast of the musical *Hair* (left) in rehearsal in September 1968, shortly before opening night at the Shaftesbury Theatre. The show had already been a hit on Broadway the previous year. It was about to take London by storm, playing to the new hippie ethos and hailing the dawning of a new Age of Aquarius in which peace would guide the planets and love would steer the stars. It was a riot of jubilant singing and nudity, and a beguiling fantasy while it lasted. Predictably the show attracted mixed reviews.

In these creatively fertile times, there was much cross-pollination between literature, the stage and cinema. Alan Sillitoe's novel *Saturday Night and Sunday Morning*, published in 1958, was filmed in 1960 starring Albert Finney. Another landmark of British realism, Shelagh Delaney's stage play *A Taste of Honey*, hit cinema screens in 1961, starring Rita Tushingham. This bittersweet story of a northern working-class girl did not flinch from issues of sexuality, race and unwanted pregnancy. Backstreet abortion featured in Nell Dunn's *Up The Junction* and in Bill Naughton's *Alfie*, which started out on radio in 1962 as 'Alfie Elkins and His Little Life'. It transferred to the stage before Michael Caine played the cockney Casanova in the definitive film version in 1966.

Along with contemporary fiction, there was a wealth of adaptations of literary classics, including Henry Fielding's *Tom Jones* and Thomas Hardy's *Far from the Madding Crowd*, starring Terence Stamp and Julie Christie, who also took the role of Lara in *Dr Zhivago*, David Lean's epic version of the Boris Pasternak novel. Ken Russell's *Women In Love*, from the D H Lawrence novel, appeared in 1969; it featured a famous nude wrestling scene with Alan Bates and Oliver Reed, but Glenda Jackson took the acting honours and the year's Oscar for Best Actress. There were some larky vehicles for the Beatles – *Help!*, *A Hard Day's Night* and *Magical Mystery Tour* – and Cliff Richard (*The Young Ones*, *Summer Holiday*). Another Swinging London piece was the cult movie *Tonite Let's All Make Love in*

SCREEN LEGENDS
Two of Britain's biggest film stars emerged in the 1960s – Sean Connery, seen here as the original James Bond, agent 007, in a scene from *Dr No* (above), and Michael Caine (right), who got his film break in the role of a British army officer in *Zulu* in 1964. Caine would really start to make his mark the following year as Harry Palmer in *The Ipcress File*, then as the eponymous, womanising anti-hero *Alfie* in 1966. Connery is still felt by most fans to be the definitive Bond, but he felt trapped and typecast by the role. He made six Bond films, the last of them, *Diamonds are Forever*, in 1971.

London, featuring appearances by David Hockney, Julie Christie and Michael Caine, with a soundtrack by Pink Floyd, the Small Faces and the Rolling Stones.

The first Bond film, *Dr No*, was released in 1962, starring Sean Connery as agent 007. Next came *From Russia With Love* (1963), then *Goldfinger* (1964). Ian Fleming took the name of his eponymous villain from Erno Goldfinger, the architect of west London high rise Trellick Tower and the much-despised Alexander Fleming House, DHSS headquarters at the Elephant and Castle. Like many people in Britain Fleming was not, it seems, a fan of modernist architecture.

INDEX

PICTURE ACKNOWLEDGEMENTS

Abbreviations: t = top; m = middle; b = bottom; r = right; c = centre; l = left

All images in this book are courtesy of Getty Images, including the following which have additional attributions:

2, 46, 58, 81: Time & Life Pictures
20, 24bl, 27, 31b, 40, 42t, 55, 70,
   78b, 79, 83, 88, 91tl, 97, 99, 110b,
   112, 119t, 120b, 134, 140, 146b,
   147r, 155: Popperfoto
29: Horst Tappe
35, 75, 135b: Steve Lewis

44, 77, 89b: GAB Archive/Redferns
45: Michael Ochs Archive
66: John Drysdale
74, 100, 103: Vernon Stratton
84: National Geographic
89t: Val Wilmer/Redferns
90: Peter Francis/Redferns

91bl: Ron Howard/Redferns
91br, 92: David Redfern/Redferns
93: Chris Morphet/Redferns
120t, 144r: Redferns
121: Terry O'Neill
144l: Chris Walter/WireImage
156: MGM Studios

LOOKING BACK AT BRITAIN
BREAKING WITH TRADITION – 1960s
is published by The Reader's Digest Association Ltd,
London, in association with Getty Images and
Endeavour London Ltd.

Copyright © 2010 The Reader's Digest Association Ltd

The Reader's Digest Association Ltd
11 Westferry Circus
Canary Wharf
London E14 4HE
www.readersdigest.co.uk

Endeavour London Ltd
21–31 Woodfield Road
London W9 2BA
info@endeavourlondon.com

Written by
Rose Shepherd

For Endeavour
Publisher: Charles Merullo
Designer: Tea Aganovic
Picture editors: Jennifer Jeffrey, Franziska Payer Crockett
Production: Mary Osborne

For Reader's Digest
Project editor: Christine Noble
Art editor: Conorde Clarke
Indexer: Marie Lorimer
Proofreader: Ron Pankhurst
Pre-press account manager: Dean Russell
Product production manager: Claudette Bramble
Production controller: Sandra Fuller

Reader's Digest General Books
Editorial director: Julian Browne
Art director: Anne-Marie Bulat

Colour origination by Chroma Graphics Ltd, Singapore
Printed and bound in China

We are committed both to the quality of our
products and the service we provide to our customers.
We value your comments, so please do contact us on
08705 113366 or via our website at
www.readersdigest.co.uk

If you have any comments or suggestions about
the content of our books, email us at
gbeditorial@readersdigest.co.uk

CONCEPT CODE: UK 0154/L/S
BOOK CODE: 638-012 UP0000-1
ISBN: 978 0 276 44400 5
ORACLE CODE: 356900012H.00.24